OUT OF COMFORT ZONE

A JOURNEY ABOUT EXPLORING YOURSELF AND BREAKING YOUR OWN LIMITS

OUT OF COMFORT ZONE

EXTENDED VERSION

CUTTING EDGE BUSINESS LESSONS BASED ON SPORTS PSYCHOLOGY FROM THE EXPERIENCE OF AN EXTREME SWIMMER

DENIZ KAYADELEN

Out of Comfort Zone

First Edition 2020
Extended Edition 2024

Published by Happy Self Publishing
www.happyselfpublishing.com
writetous@happyselfpublishing.com

HAPPY
SELF PUBLISHING

Table of Contents

Acknowledgments

Everything in our lives is there for a reason and shapes us in our journey in one way or another. Our journey starts when we are born and ends when we die. What matters is what we do on our defined path and in our environment where we are born, grow up, and which roads we select. I am so grateful to all the people in my life who have shown me the right direction, starting with my parents and continuing with my friends and colleagues.

Everything I have done and achieved in my life wouldn't have happened without my parents, family, and broader support system. Every person in my life showed me something, and I am really grateful for that.

Every achievement you read here is part of their success as well.

On this road, I had, of course, failures and losses. My support system sometimes gave me hints that I didn't follow. I take all the responsibility for all my failures and losses. Actually, I do not believe in the words failure or loss. Because, at that moment, it was the right or best thing that I was capable of doing or thinking. That's why I stopped judging myself or regretting my past actions, which may not have led to success or a happy end. These actions are part of myself. I welcome them and try to learn from them to be a better person and athlete. I want to give thanks to all those painful moments as well, which have given me the power I have and shaped me into who I am and how I think.

I want to first thank my mom. She always pushed me, loved me, gave me the courage to continue even when I felt sad or exhausted. We were a rich family, and my mom was the person who always told me that I needed to trust myself, my own skills, and not rely on others for success. Even when I was four or five, she spoke to me like an adult and gave me the respect and love that I needed. She pushed my swimming and my career and supported me through my life as a single mother. Even if she didn't want that I swim the dangerous routes, she was still with me, believed in me, and sent her love. *"Love you, mum!"*

My dad was a strong man who respected my decisions and believed in me. He always showed his pride and gave me the courage to continue, both in my career and at swimming. In my childhood, he was sometimes too disciplined and showed less emotion, but he always respected me and gave me the power to make my own decisions and continue with my own life. He showed me the analytical and realistic part of life. He inspired me with his dedication, strongness, and never give up mentality. *"Love you, Dad."*

Thank you, my cousin, Yasin, who introduced me to one of my best friends, Emre Deliveli. Emre was my relay swim mate, who supported me in realizing my dreams, such as swimming the English Channel- and now publishing this book. My cold-water journey started with him- and will continue with further projects that will come soon. We swam together, we cried together, we fought together, and we laughed together. He has been in my life for only two years but contributed to all the highlights and supported me to the fullest. *"Lucky, to have you in my life. Thank you, Emre!"*

My first coach, Ali Birinci, motivated and supported me all the time. Thank you, Ali, for being with me in my hard times and supporting me to become a good swimmer.

My swimming friends are like my family members. It is an amazing feeling to not just swim with them, but also enjoy the before and after swimming ceremonies like chilling, speaking, and eating together. They are always with me in and out of the water. There are my pacemakers, motivators in the water. Thank you, Kristian Schneider, Boris Konopka, Rainer Zettl, Torsten, for the great swim sessions in the pool and lakes and for the great times out of the water.

Thank you, Bakirkoy Ata Su Sporlari Swimming Club and Sait Babaoglu, who supported me in my swim challenges of the English Channel and North Channel and managed my media channels and relations.

Thank you, Enver Alas, who has been dedicated in supporting me in the Turkish news.

My childhood friends from swimming are special to me. Asli Eter was always with me during hard times when I moved from Germany to Turkey. We swam together in the Yesilyurt swimming team and became close friends. Even in lockdown, we trained together, doing cross-fit via Zoom and motivating each other. "Thank you for being with me no matter where and when, Asli! You really are the one person who understands my soul and me!"

My schoolteacher, Prof. Murat Beken, motivated and supported me during my high school. He believed in me, and with his mentorship, I became the school's top student in the school. *"Thank you for your encouragement and mentorship!"*

My university professor, Heinrich Wottawa, always asked me challenging questions, coached me, and supported me during my master's, and thanks to him, I found my first job. He always understood me, saw my deeper soul, and gave me the right advice at the right time. *"Thank you, Prof. Wottawa, for your guidance, support, and challenging questions, which pushed me out of my comfort zone and encouraged me to take action in my life."*

Thank you, my uncles, and greater family members. Without them, we wouldn't have gone every summer to our family summer holiday place and swum together in the beautiful sea.

Thanks, my family; I had a great childhood, with a feeling of belongingness.

Thank you, my team members, Yasemin Bagana, Emre Deliveli, and our coach Kamil Resa Alsaran. With you as a team, I could go out of my comfort zone and do those amazing relay swims of the English Channel and North Channel, becoming part of the first Turkish team that crossed the North Channel. Also with this team I could swim the English Channel solo.

Thank you to my English Channel sponsor Adalvo and to Fitline for the nutrition support. Your support is really appreciated. Thank you Speedo for the equipment support. The more I go for my dreams the more I feel the support of those amazing companies.

Introduction

Are you a swimmer, an athlete, a businessperson who wants to go one step further, explore your limits what you are capable of? Are you a person who searches for the purpose of life and wants to find and follow their passion? Do you want to use your failures or pain as a chance for growth? Are you ready to go out of your comfort zone to explore yourself in another dimension and break your limits? If your answer to any of the above is "yes," you should continue reading this book.

This book describes a journey about life, about being out of the comfort zone, and how we break our limits and grow physically and mentally. There are no limits to what you can accomplish except the limits you place on your own thinking. Writing and publishing a book is an out of comfort zone experience for me, and I can't believe I have found the courage to write these lines, especially in English, which is not my mother tongue. I have waited for further immersive experiences, further growth stories. But then, I recognized there is no limit to growth and no limit to what you can accomplish and there is no limit to choosing the next level of challenge in your life. I am now sitting here in Johannesburg, South Africa, for a business assignment during the Covid-19 pandemic lockdown. I'm at home, thinking about how I can transform this pain of sitting and working at home, with all the ups and downs, to a better dimension by finding myself, reflecting on my life and thoughts and sharing those and my stories and experiences with you. I forget when this lockdown started, I do not know when it might end. I am just focusing on the now, on this moment, and feeling the flow, reflecting on my thoughts. What I want to highlight is that all these stories and achievements are not just mine. I may have forced it and become the main part of it, but this is a shared journey, a joint achievement. Without my family, friends, and coaches, I wouldn't be sitting here and writing these lines.

My name is Deniz, which means sea in Turkish. My destiny with water was decided before I was born. I am a Business Psychologist, Coach, Trainer, and Manager at one of the Big Four accounting firms (Along with Deloitte, KPMG, and PricewaterhouseCoopers) and Ernst & Young, known simply as EY. EY is a multinational professional services firm headquartered in London, England, United Kingdom, and it is one of the largest professional services firms in the world. It primarily provides assurance (which includes financial audit), tax, consulting, and advisory services to its clients. I work in the people advisory area, supporting clients in people-related issues in business and managing different change - transformation and talent management related projects. I consult for clients to find the answers in the areas of: What is the right place and position for the right talent? How can transformation affect companies, and how can people be educated and motivated for future requirements in the new normal?

Besides that, I am an extreme swimmer and have tried continuing my swimming despite my busy consulting life. I am not an extraordinary person who will tell you about the perfect world or about perfection itself. My aim is to share my experiences and inspirational sources with you, with the hope that I can touch your heart and give you a piece of inspiration to increase your courage to follow your passion and chart your own journey by going out of your comfort zone and expanding your growth zone.

Life is never easy; it has never been easy. Pain and discomfort are parts of our life. The ups and downs are part of our journey, which lead to growth. We start our lives by crying and continue with many challenges in different areas of our lives. We, as human beings, have different needs. Our psychological needs, such as to be loved, accepted, heard, deemed important, to belong to someone, are never fulfilled to the fullest from our childhood, and those internal gaps cause pain as well as external circumstances. Of course, we do not plan our life to feel pain or discomfort. It happens suddenly and unplanned. And it comes when you have the courage to leave your comfort zone for further experiences. Without pain and discomfort, you can't know comfort and happiness. Without breaking your own limits, you cannot explore yourself and fulfill your potential to the fullest. It is not that you cannot do something you dream of, it's just that maybe, you can't do it or achieve it YET.

Without trying, you'll never know how it feels and what you are capable of. OUT OF YOUR COMFORT ZONE IS YOUR GROWTH ZONE AND WILL BECOME YOUR NEW COMFORT ZONE AFTER YOUR INDIVIDUAL TRANSFORMATION. Your transformation begins with discomfort and your way of dealing with it.

Outside comfort areas, such as challenging moments with family or work, some people choose to be victims, and others choose to be heroes or fighters with the aim of growing stronger from these situations. In which category are you and which do you want to be in in your near future?

1

Which zones are familiar to you, and in which zone are you in at the moment?

Most of the time, outside of your comfort zone is the zone where we feel unsafe because of the higher risk of failing or being overwhelmed. But in this zone, we are learning to overcome our fears, finding out how to deal with our limiting beliefs and inner blocks. Our individual growth comes from pain and a step-by-step transformation processes; from a fear zone to a growth zone, from an out of comfort zone to comfort zone. The out of comfort zone becomes our new comfort zone through our individual growth zone.

We are moving from one zone to another. Sometimes, we are aware of the zones, and sometimes, it is an unconscious process where we feel comfortable or less safe and confident. The more you understand the concept, the better you can reflect and control your inner zones, observe the zones of others, and handle those, both in your private and corporate life, much better and more effectively. Understanding yourself is the first step to understanding others.

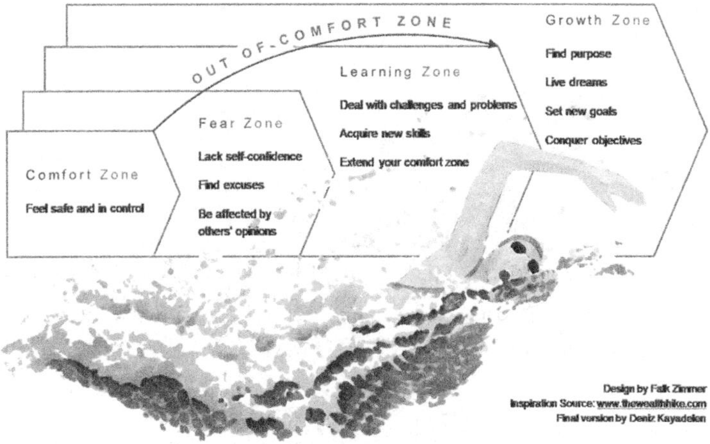

THERE ARE FIVE MAIN ZONES

First, the most comfortable area is our Comfort Zone:
We need our comfort zone, where we feel safe and know what we are doing, feeling the control and confidence in our lives. This zone is where we regenerate ourselves, to have time to rest and save our strength for facing potential challenges in different zones. To be safe and feeling comfortable are two of our basic needs. Everybody has their own comfort zone. Some feel in their comfort zone when they are at home and cooking, and for some, it's working in the office and getting a promotion based on the hard and well-deserved work. The definition is different for everyone. You can reflect on your own comfort zone; this is important for you to know to use the zones properly in your life. The risk of the comfort zone is that you may not be learning new things; you are experiencing more routines and could easily get bored. Routine is predictable. It is comfortable, but it is also a zone where we are moving less, transforming our mind and body to another level less.

The second one is the Out of Comfort Zone, where the fear zone starts and continues with the learning and growth zones. This zone is between the comfort and growth zones. Without stepping out of the comfort zone, you can't reach the growth zone, which is again a comfort area in a higher dimension. When we are in the growth zone, we are directly expanding our comfort zone and feel safer and less anxious. This is a sign that we are getting stronger and transforming ourselves. But before we do this, we need to go through the fear zone.

Outside of our comfort zone is the most unpredictable and insecure area in our life. The more we have the courage to face the unknown, the more we grow and explore our limits. We see what we can handle; we feel our potential and break our boundaries by transforming ourselves—transforming our mind, our body, and our behaviors.

The third one is our Fear Zone: Fear is an emotion induced by perceived danger or threat, which causes physiological, and ultimately, behavioral changes, such as hiding, fleeing, or freezing from perceived distressing actions. Anxiety or fear in human beings may occur as a reaction to stimulus happening in the present, or in anticipation or expectation of a future threat. The more we have bad associations, for example, from our childhood or latest undesirable experiences, the more we face our fears. Sometimes, we just want to be in the comfort zone and don't want to go out of this zone because of our inner blockades, especially our fears. In the fear zone, most of the time, we find excuses for not trying new things, feeling a lack of self-confidence, and are more affected by the opinions of others or limiting beliefs. In this zone, the anxiety level is high. The more we feel anxiety the more we feel blocks in our inner thought process and feel less courage to do something or try something new. Most of the time, when we hear from others, "Don't do this, it's dangerous, it's too risky, or you can't do it," it's based on their own bad associations and limiting beliefs, which could also come from their own inner fears and blockades. This is the most vulnerable phase. We do not feel safe, and we want to leave this zone. We want to survive, and our brain tries to convince us to move back to our comfort zone.

The fourth one is the Learning Zone: In the learning zone, we are willing to deal with challenges and problems, learn new things, and explore ourselves. If we are not feeling challenged or fearful, we will not learn to overcome those feelings and situations. We are exploring ourselves through new experiences, expanding our way of thinking, and going one step further. This is the zone where we learn new things, gain more self-confidence by facing our fears and overcoming them.

The fifth one is the Growth Zone: In the growth zone, we are setting new goals and finding a purpose for our life. We reflect and identify the reason why we are alive and what we want to stand for. In this zone, we live our dreams by going out of our comfort zone and facing magical moments. Our brain and body are faced with new stimulations, and this state is also activating the reward system and adrenaline in our body.

In this book, I want to share my journey in these zones, with focus on the out of comfort and growth zones. I will concentrate on my swimming journey and some personal life stories, combining them with insights from my professional and educational background.

SUMMARY

1. **Most of the time, outside of our comfort zone is the zone where we feel unsafe** because of the higher risk of failing or being overwhelmed. But in this zone, we are learning to overcome our fears, finding out how to deal with our limiting beliefs and inner blocks. Our individual growth comes from pain and step-by-step transformation processes.

2. **There are five main zones, in which we are moving from one zone to another:**
   - ▶ Comfort Zone
   - ▶ Out of Comfort Zone
   - ▶ Fear Zone
   - ▶ Learning Zone
   - ▶ Growth Zone

3. **The more you understand the concept of those zones, the better you can reflect and control your inner zones,** observe the zones of others, and handle those both in your private and corporate life much better and more effectively.

4. **Understanding yourself is the first step to understanding others.**

2

Every goodbye is a new start – From the fear zone to the learning zone

FROM GERMANY TO TURKEY – JULY 1998

Sometimes, everything comes at once, and you have the feeling of being overwhelmed. Many challenges are forcing you to face them all at once. I cannot forget the year when I was eleven years old.

It started with a skiing accident, where I broke two parts of my arm, damaged my ribs, and even risked losing my kidney. I crashed head-on into a wall. It was like in a movie. People, including my mom, watched the exact moment it happened. I lost control, couldn't see anything, closed my eyes, and I crashed… into the wall at very high speed. I remember that I couldn't breathe, couldn't talk, couldn't move. My skis flew in two different directions. I only heard people and felt them as they came to check on me and listened to the siren of the ambulance. They had come to save me. I trusted them and hoped to be able to speak, breathe, and move my body again soon.

After two emergency operations, the doctors in Germany and Turkey saved my kidney and arm. After six weeks, I could go to school again and continue with my routine life. Did I say routine life?

When I came back home, I recognized that there was no way back anymore in terms of our "normal" happy and peaceful family life. I was the only child, and my mom and dad were not the perfect couple. But I had always hoped that they could find a peaceful way to be together. After a few weeks, I recognized that things were changing fast.

One day, my mom came to me and said, "we are moving to Turkey. You and me." That was the moment I felt, for the first time, the most significant loss of my life. We were also having financial problems, so we lost our family life as well as our family-owned business; I lost my friends, the country where I was born, and much more. I lost the language I had spoken since birth; I lost my ballet classes; I lost my swim lessons; I lost my daily, weekly, and monthly routines. I lost everything. That was, of course, in my mind. But it was not just in my mind. Somehow, it was reality. I needed to cope with this reality of losing everything I had so far. I felt the pain of my mom. I felt the pain of my dad. I felt the pain of my body and mind. But I knew there was no way back anymore. I needed to cope with the situation with my family. I needed to cope with myself. I needed to cope with the environment. I needed to say goodbye. Goodbye to everything that I loved, that I was used to.

At the same time, this goodbye was a new start for all of us.

Every goodbye is a new welcome for surprises!

I decided to say hello to everything, to my new life. Hello to a fresh start with many surprises, many new people, a new language, a new school, new friends, a new social environment. And of course, hello to the beautiful metropolis of Istanbul, truly a world city, which everyone should visit at least once in their lifetime. It is an enchanting blend of Eastern and Western culture, a vibrant, modern city with a unique identity. I was overwhelmed, but at the same time, curious about the city, about the people, and everything that was waiting for me.

WHO COULD KNOW THAT MY PASSION BEGAN WITH MY BIGGEST ENEMY – HOW I STARTED MY SWIM JOURNEY

The first step was to find a new home in Istanbul. We were lucky and found a beautiful home in a gorgeous area near the sea called Yesilkoy. The next challenge was to find a German-speaking school. We figured out everything and settled down in a short period. It was a complete out of comfort zone experience for me. My dad and my friends, the people whom I was used to, were not with me anymore. The culture was completely different. The language was different. The environment had different expectations, and I needed to introduce myself to new people, with my own sad story in my mind.

My school was a German-speaking school, but some courses were still in Turkish. I remember the math class, where I didn't even know the word for triangle in Turkish. It was a challenge to understand everything and continue as if nothing had happened.

After school in the afternoons, when I came home, almost every day I heard the same story. Our story. Our sad story about why we moved from Germany to Turkey. My mom was sad; she was annoyed and frustrated, which was normal and understandable after a divorce. For me, as a child, it was hard to handle all the challenges at school and home. It broke my heart, every day, to see my mom at home and not see her smiling. With my dad, I had little contact.

I tried to stay strong for my future and my mom. She promised me that, together, we would figure everything out and continue stronger than before with our new life. Most of the time, I felt alone and a little bit lost in life. Despite relatives and my new friends at school, something was missing. My whole life had changed - the way I went to school, the way I ate and slept, my social environment.

A few months later, it was time to find a new hobby, which would make me happy again, give me a feeling of empowerment, more trust in what was going on around me, and the feeling of belonging somewhere strongly as well as help me find deeper connections.

Near our house, there was a highly renowned sports club. My mom had been a member before she had moved to Germany and still knew many people from the old times. We decided to check the options for me.

In Germany, I had many hobbies. My schedule was busy every day with tennis, ballet, piano lessons, and swimming. I enjoyed swimming the most. Every time I was in the water, I felt I was in a different world. I felt the water intensely, going to another dimension, and after swimming, I felt, every time, like a new-born, free and happy. Swimming took all my negative energy into the water and gave me a feeling of freedom and power.

So I decided to start swimming, and I joined one of the best swimming clubs in Turkey. There were different levels from A to D. A team was the fastest team, and D had beginners in their group. The trainer checked my swimming skills and decided to put me in level A. That meant five days of training every week.

Oh no. Is that true? I did not enjoy doing so much sport at all. Sport wasn't a focus of my life. I was generally lazy and always preferred to go somewhere by car or take the elevator rather than the stairs. This was another big challenge in my life. I already had enough to handle, and now I had to deal with hectic training sessions with my tired mind and lazy body.

In Germany, I had enjoyed swimming, but only once a week, with no racing goals or intense training sessions. Now, I was in this swimming team and needed to train five days a week. NO way!

The first training sessions were really frustrating for me. Everybody was faster. I felt like a loser; I didn't feel the power in my body. I pushed myself, but my body and my mind were tired. I had mixed feelings about swimming. On the one hand, I was in a great team with friendly people and a perfect trainer and belonged to a group. On the other hand, I felt too tired and overwhelmed; I just wanted to go home after school, not to practice.

I remember my first swim weeks. One day, the training was so hard that I got out of the water and started crying like a small kid. I felt so embarrassed but couldn't stop myself. I felt so frustrated with my life, with my mind, my body, and everything. I felt so weak. I couldn't handle the situation and found the solution by getting out of the water and crying. When I went home, I told my mom that I didn't want to go swimming anymore. It was just too stressful and overwhelming. I could not endure this demanding performance, and I just wanted to stay at home and do nothing. I knew that if I went to training fewer than four times a week, they would kick me out of the A team. My mom listened to me and kept silent.

The day after, she spoke to my trainer, without letting me know, and asked him for a few weeks of tolerance. She believed that I would continue with swimming when I didn't feel under pressure.

One week later, I went home and asked my mom if I should go swimming or not. She said, "It is your choice. If you want to stay at home, you can. If you want to go, you can go." I needed to continue, that I needed to face this challenge and my fears and feelings, which caused me to feel weak.

I decided to go to training that day. This training was the last training that I ever had doubts about. After this day, my life changed. I felt the internal motivation to start swimming properly. I was ready to continue, to go one step ahead, knowing that I needed to train a lot and needed a lot of mental power to become better and faster to feel comfortable within this amazing, fast-performing team.

I accepted the challenge and decided to continue swimming. It was at least a real start. A start to my inner journey, a start to my passion, a start to getting stronger from situations where I felt bad or weak. A start for my individual transformation to see challenges as a chance for my individual growth.

I went swimming seven times a week. In the winter, it was five times in the afternoons and twice in the mornings at 5.30 am. It required discipline, mental and physical power, determination, and inner motivation. In the summer, we swam outside in a beautiful 25-meter saltwater pool with a sea view. We swam every day, except Mondays when we swam twice a day. The swimming team became my new extended family. My trainer was like my big brother, and my swim mates were my sisters and brothers. I strongly felt that I belonged to those great people and the water.

The real fight begins after you feel pain and discomfort, and you can be a winner when you manage your pain and continue despite your inner blocks

Some training sessions were hard and pushed our limits. One day, we needed to swim twenty-one-hundred meters at the same fast pace, with just 20-second breaks in between. After the seventh one, I felt so exhausted and just wanted to drink water, missing the start of the eighth one. Our trainer got very angry and kicked me out of the training session and out of the pool. I felt so bad and was so angry with him. He had hurt me. I was a disciplined swimmer, and he just ignored this and showed his power to kick me out in front of so many other swimmers and trainers. A few days later, we spoke about this, and he said, "No matter how tired you are, no matter how exhausted you feel, you always need to continue. The real fight begins after you feel pain and discomfort. You can be a winner when you manage your pain and continue despite your inner blocks." He wanted to make me feel uncomfortable to give this life lesson to me. I accepted it and understood what he was saying to me. After this time, every time I felt tired or wanted to stop, I thought about this incident and reminded myself to continue what I was doing.

The brain is so powerful. With your brain, you can control your body, the pain, and push your endurance to the fullest.

Swimming has taught me so many things and has given me a feeling of freedom and power. Even if I have a bad day or mood, after 30 minutes of swimming, I transform into a meditative mood and forget everything around me. After a 1 to 1.5-hour training session, I feel exhausted but happy. Swimming has taught me to be and stay disciplined. I am not an early bird and enjoy sleeping until 8 am. Those morning training sessions taught me to wake up despite my inner blocks and desire to sleep. Afterward, I was always grateful to have had the opportunity to start my day in such a great way. I felt energized for the rest of the day and could concentrate much better at school.

After several months of rigorous training, I became one of the fastest members of the team and started participating in the Turkish championships every year. My favorite style was the butterfly, and I trained hard to learn the technique properly. I pushed myself to swim the cool-down sets and had some days where I swam more than 1.5 km of butterfly in total. After a few years, I swam in the Turkish finals of the 200-meter butterfly and was one of the five fastest women in Turkey in my age category.

SUMMARY

1. **Every challenge brings you one step further in your life and shapes your personality.** It makes you the person you are now. Your experiences and how you handle your challenges have a huge impact on your thought process and character. See those challenges as a chance to shape your personality in a positive way and grow.

2. **Don't forget every end is a new start.** Life always comes with surprises, embrace them and don't be afraid to leave your old habits and environment.

3. **Find and follow your passion.** Sometimes it's not clear, and maybe your biggest enemy or fear can become your real passion.

4. **The real fight begins after you feel pain and discomfort**. You can be a winner when you manage your pain and continue despite your inner blocks such us feelings like fear, demotivation, frustration.

5. **Your brain is so powerful. Use it!** With your brain, you can control your body, the pain, and push your endurance to the fullest. You can realize everything that you want with your brainpower and hard work.

6. **Every journey has its own reason.** Try to make the most of it and transform the pain into chances for your life. See everything as a sign and a further milestone for your individual growth and happiness in your individual journey.

3

Meeting my real love and passion in the sea

HOW DID I START WITH OPEN WATER SWIMMING?

My swim journey started in the pool and continued in the sea. My open water swim passion started in paradise. My family had a summer house in Datça, a town in the Muğla Province in southwestern Turkey, between the well-known resort towns of Bodrum and Marmaris. We were there every summer, and I used the opportunity to find my real passion in the water.

Datça, my favorite place in the world... The place where I feel peace and close to nature; it's where I can hear my inner voice. Datça is the place where I started open water swimming 20 years ago. It is also the place where I started to meditate and motivate my body and mind to go out of my comfort zone. It is hard to explain how this place gives me a natural strength.

Datça has the best weather in Turkey, and it's a place of peace and natural beauty. The spindly, 50-mile-long Datça peninsula is a dagger of pure green at the meeting point of the Aegean and the Mediterranean. The ancient Greeks believed Datça to have been created by Zeus, so gorgeous are its rocky outcrops and aquamarine waters. The geographer Strabo apparently said: "God sent his beloved creatures to Datça for them to live longer." Every summer, we went there, and all the extended family members met there. I have quite a big family. It was a meeting point for all my cousins and uncles, and we all have great memories in this paradise.

My family, like me, loves nature and sports. Our day started at 7 am, with trekking around 10 kilometers in the beautiful mountains. On one road, you can see on the Mediterranean Sea on the left side and the Aegean Sea on the right. Amazing views and the smell of nature, such as thymine, sage, and jasmine flowers pervades the area.

After our trekking tour, we rewarded ourselves with fresh watermelons and figs from our farm. And what was next? Of course, going into the sea and swimming for as long as we could before our family brunch-kind-of-breakfast around lunchtime.

I can say with confidence that Datça has the most beautiful seawater in the world. The temperature is always a little bit colder compared to other places in the same region, around 22 degrees in the summertime. The water is clean. There is no dangerous sea wildlife. The sea has strong waves, especially in the afternoon; you can feel the power of nature in the water through the strong currents and waves.

Every summer, I swam in the mornings after trekking and in the afternoons after sunbathing on my favorite small island. I swam every day for around eight kilometers in total. In the morning, five kilometers and three kilometers in the afternoon.

I started to enjoy the waves, to feel the different moods of the water in the morning and the afternoon. The waves and the currents gave me joy, and I felt the natural power and freedom in the water. The expression of the sea was unbelievable. It was a completely different feeling compared to the pool. I realized that open water was my real passion. When I was in the water, I wanted to go further and further. I didn't feel any fear, even when I went alone to the deepest part of the bay, where you couldn't see the bottom of the sea. I felt that I belonged to the sea and the sea to me. We, as human beings, are also like seawater. I reflect on the parallelism and feel the connection between my body, my soul, and my mind with the limitless ocean. The color, the salty taste, the feeling of the waves… I love everything about the sea. It's like an endless relationship between the sea and me. An endless and unconditional love. A real love that I feel with all my body, soul, and mind. Sometimes wavy, sometimes calm, sometimes unpredictable.

The holiday in Datça was kind of a sports camp for me. Besides swimming, I ran on the beach, walked in the mountains, and did some cross-fit exercises. I thought of using this momentum to join the national and international open water races.

Open water swimming is an entirely different challenge compared to the pool. For one thing, all pools are more or less the same: The distance is 25 or 50 meters. The temperature varies from 24 to 28 degrees. There are no waves, no surprises during your race. And of course, you need to be able to do flip turns really well.

Of course, you don't need to do flip turns in open water swims. But there are even bigger differences between the two: In the open water, no two swims are alike, even the same route during different times of the day. Currents, waves, weather, wind, and water temperature all play a role. And of course, if you are doing a swim longer than 5K, eating and drinking during the swim will be very important. Datça gave me the power and experience to deal with all those uncertainties in the water and the courage to attend open water races.

SUMMARY

1. **Reflect and find your real passion.** If you don't know it today, it's ok. Keep searching, exploring, until you feel it. Your inner voice will tell you what you enjoy and what makes you really happy.

2. **Don't worry if you don't find your passion immediately.** There are so many new activities that you can explore, and when you have the flow experience, enjoying the time, feeling the inner motivation to continue, feeling recharged and happy, then you know that you have found your passion.

3. **Find your favorite place in life**. The location, where you feel comfortable and regenerate yourself will give you the feeling of relaxation, and you will recharge yourself for further challenges in your way.

4. **Take time to feel nature, feel yourself, and follow your passion.** Breathe, reflect, and don't rush. It's ok to take time for yourself and your thought process. You don't always need to be in action. Find time to relax in nature, feel what's happening, and do what is really good for you.

4

Open water races in Turkey A dream come true

HOW I HAD FIRST PLACE BY SWIMMING FROM ASIA TO EUROPE

My first open water race was one of the biggest international swim events in the world, where you swim from Asia to Europe. The **Bosporus Cross Continental** Swim is an open water swimming event between the continents Europe and Asia held annually in Istanbul, usually at the end of July. While more than 2,400 competitors from across the globe take over the Bosporus waters, one of the busiest shipping lanes in the world is temporarily closed to traffic for three hours. You can't believe how amazing it is to swim under the bridge that connects Europe to Asia and see the beautiful views and houses in the center of Istanbul. The race starts in the Asian neighborhood of Kanlica and ends in the European district of Kurucesme. The distance is about 6 km. The current is strong, and besides endurance and speed, you also need a really good feeling and knowledge of the route and the areas and directions of the currents. In my first race, I came 4th in my age category. I wasn't prepared for this race mentally.

One year later, I analyzed the route, prepared a tactic in my mind, studied the different directions of the currents on a detailed map. The Bosphorous is really tricky. There are two different currents going in opposite directions. When you are too far to the left or right, you have the current against you, and when you swim exactly in the middle of the channel, you have the current behind, which supports you and pushes you toward the finish.

There is a small manmade island called Galatasaray Island, a short distance from the finish. In my first race, I swam directly to the finish line after the island, and it was the biggest mistake I could ever make in this race. Many swimmers are trapped between the island and the finish line behind it. Even if you are a fast swimmer, you can't swim against the strong current there. You must feel and understand nature and follow its rules. You can't fight against nature. You need to dance with the waves, with the wind, and follow the signs nature is giving you. Like in our normal life as well, isn't it?

In my second race, I learned from this experience and decided to prepare myself more mentally and prepare a tactic for my route.

When I saw the same island, I continued to swim straight even though the route was going to be longer, I used the power of nature, the currents, turning to the finish area in an L-shape instead of swimming directly there. When I finished the race, I got out, and all the camera guys surrounded me, asking how I felt and what my next goal would be. I said that my goal was to be the fastest woman in my age category, without knowing that I was already the fastest woman within all age categories.

I gave some interviews and then checked the racing results after a few minutes. Unbelievably, I saw my name on top within all age categories. I was the fastest woman!

A few hours later, the ceremony began, and I cried from happiness. The moment I recognized that I had first place was unreal. I hugged my friends, my trainer, my mom, and had a sense of flying. In addition to the physical preparation, the mental preparation had helped me to become the fastest woman in this amazing race in just one year.

This experience showed me that when our mental and physical power go in the same direction, and when we are fully prepared for something, there are no limits to what we are capable of. After winning this race, I started to believe in my inner potential more, and a new dimension opened in my mind and body. I decided to use this potential and join further events in my element – the open water.

One race followed another, and I won many open water races as the fastest woman overall.

One of those amazing races was the **Canakkale Marathon**, which is on Turkey's Victory Day. The Dardanelles Strait is closed to maritime traffic for 1½ hours while swimmers race the 4.5km from Eceabat to Çanakkale. I won first place overall for three consecutive years. Quantum watches were the sponsors during that time, and as a winner, I got beautiful Quantum watches. But they gave me men's watches instead of women's all the time. After giving my awards to my dad and my boyfriend at the time, I took my watch to their headquarters in the third year and asked to replace my prize with a women's model. In the end, I could wear my own watch, which I had won through swimming.

SWIMMING FOR PEACE

Another great race was to swim for peace between Turkey and Greece. The **Meis-Kaş marathon**, from the harbor of the Greek island of Castellorizo to Kaş Harbor in Turkey, is a distance of around 8 kilometers. I was happy to be the fastest open water swimmer in Turkey again and enjoyed every moment of the preparation, training, and experiences with my teammates. We had fun, we had pain, we experienced many emotions at once, and those kinds of moments made our relationships stronger.

I also continued with the rigorous pool training 5 to 8 times a week and the national races until the university preparation year.

THE TOUGHEST YEAR -PREPARATION FOR THE UNIVERSITY EXAM - 2013 - 2014

The period of preparing for the university exam, which is called OSS, is one of the most challenging times for many young Turks. This exam is a standardized test for admission to higher education institutions in Turkey. Within the Turkish education system, the only way to enter a university is through this exam, which encompasses all the work of a student through their 12 years of academic life into a 3-hour multiple-choice exam. More than 2,000,000 high school graduates take the multiple-choice format exam every year, which has 180 questions and measures analytical as well as verbal skills.

In effect, the score on the test defines your future. Based on the score, you can choose your preferred universities and majors. You have a top ten list, and depending on the demand and supply, the system automatically places you in one of your choices. That means your future, your destiny, is a little bit in the hands of the system, and if you are lucky, you will be placed in one of your top choices.

In this preparation period, I stopped swimming, but I continued with underwater hockey so that I would not be too far away from the water. I had training every two weeks. It was fun; I still felt the water and was still able to do something for my body and mind.

The grades in school affected the overall university entrance score as well. That's why I put my success at school in front of my swimming. I studied every day, did my homework, and engaged proactively in my school, with the goal of being the school's top student. All my efforts throughout the years helped, and I was the **top student** in my high school in the end. This result gave me a little bit of advantage for my overall university entrance exam score. I did everything to maximize my chances to realize my dream - to be a psychologist.

SUMMARY

1. **Always dream and think big!** Set your goals high and work for that. You are more than you think, and you will see and feel it in the process more and more.

2. **Besides working hard, you need to act smart and always have a strategy.** Before you start the challenge, you need to plan, define your win strategy, define your unique selling points, understand the challenges, and plan how you face those challenges.

3. **Work hard; believe in yourself.** Continue, despite the pain, and you will succeed! Pain is a sign of pushing your limits and going out of your comfort zone. When you feel discomfort, it's a great sign of your growth, and it pushes you to achieve your goals and realize your dreams.

5

From swimming to psychology

FROM PAIN TO SUCCESS – MY JOURNEY TO PSYCHOLOGY AND BEING A (BUSINESS) PSYCHOLOGIST

I wanted to be a psychologist because I knew I couldn't earn enough money from swimming in the long run. Swimming is more of an individual sport, and there are fewer spectators and sponsors compared to popular team sports. Of course, I could choose to be a trainer and share my experiences with younger generations, but I also wanted to use my intellect and expand my horizon. I was always interested in psychology since my childhood days. I wanted to understand people's behavior, needs, and reactions. Maybe, the troubled relationship between my mom and dad pushed me in this direction as well. I was even reading psychology and philosophy books at the age of twelve or thirteen. My mom was reading those kinds of books as well, so there were plenty lying around the house, which attracted me and increased my interest in this field.

I prepared for the university exam day and night. I went to a private exam preparation course every day after school and even on weekends. I basically had no private life and was simply focused on achieving my goal and realizing my dream of being a psychologist. It was a tense year with many challenges and uncertainties.

After one year of intense preparations, and more than six years of disciplined school life as the top student in the school, I entered for the university exam.

You can't imagine how hard it was to wait for the results. My future depended on this exam. It would determine what I would become.

Three months later, I got the results. I was so nervous. I was afraid of failing, afraid not to be placed in one of my top choices! I was selected for one of the best universities in Turkey, the first public university from the Ottoman times - Istanbul University. I was so happy and felt relieved. The pressure disappeared. I started to have more hope in my life than ever and couldn't wait to become a psychologist.

As soon as I knew I had secured my place as a psychology student, I returned to swimming. Many swimmers stop after entering university because it is difficult to swim and study or swim and work at the same time. During my university years, I continued swimming, attended all my classes, and did more than five internships in forensic medicine, clinical psychology, human resources, and coaching, to understand the different aspects of psychology better and explore my real passion in this field. I worked in a psychiatry center with drug addicts, in forensic medicine, interviewing murderers, in a hospital with schizophrenic patients, and in a corporate health company in the Human Resources department.

Toward the end of my studies, I applied to study in Bochum, Germany, to do a double degree in Psychology. I applied for the Socrates Erasmus Program, and in the end, I got a double diploma in Psychology from both Germany and Turkey. The diploma from both countries was important for me because I couldn't decide where I wanted to live. I had always felt in between the two countries and, therefore, wanted to feel safe.

Based on my experiences during the internships, I felt the business world attracted me more than clinical psychology. I liked the focus on people's potentials and strengths, which I found to be more future-oriented rather than studying people's past and deeper individual problems.

That's why I decided to continue with a master's in business and organizational psychology. Business psychology focuses on issues in the corporate world, such as training and coaching of people for both individual and professional growth, assessing people for the right job or role, supporting people in change processes, and motivating people for performance improvement.

Why didn't I stop swimming and find excuses, such as being busy with studying, internships, and my social life? Because I wanted it, I needed it, and I managed my time toward it.

SUMMARY

1. **Explore until you know what you really want in life, and then go for it!**

2. **Reflect on yourself,** your needs, and know what you really want to become in your life and what your priorities are.

3. **You can't achieve anything that you really, truly don't want to achieve.** You need to want it, and when you really feel convinced, then nothing can stop you. Even if you feel pain, frustration, or fear, the power of willingness will be dominating, and all the energies in your life will support you to achieve what you really want.

4. **Dedication, desire, and commitment are key to continue things you like and to be successful besides hard work.**

5. **Your mindset is key!** Maybe you are the most talented person in one field, but if you do not have the desire, the dedication, and the willingness to commit yourself, you will not achieve the highest level of success.

6

Consulting career and competitive sports

NOTHING IS IMPOSSIBLE! IF YOU REALLY WANT SOMETHING AND WORK FOR IT, NOTHING IS IMPOSSIBLE!

After my master's, I started my career in consulting. I loved to face new challenges, the variety of different projects, and the dynamics of consulting. I knew that consulting would be a tough life. It's not a nine to five job, and you need to be ready to travel often. There is no routine, the work is not repetitive, and you always need to be creative when it comes to solving different customer issues. It's a client business. You end up going where the client is located. You are on the client's site most of the time, which means that you are staying in fancy hotels but with less time for yourself. You are often out of your comfort zone. Clients are always coming up with new challenges, and you need to solve those as a consultant. That means you need to handle difficult situations, deal with completely new topics and different kinds of personalities, and quickly learn to deliver your consulting services and add value. You need to have a unique selling point as a consultant, and it is never easy to position yourself as an expert, especially when you face new topics you are not familiar with.

FROM ISTANBUL TO BOCHUM AND FROM BOCHUM TO STUTTGART

I moved to Stuttgart for my first job, which was a big change and a completely new environment. At this time, I didn't know anyone in this new city, didn't have people to trust, and everything was new to me. My friends were in Istanbul, Berlin, and other cities. I decided to join a fitness club to stay fit and maybe meet some new people. After six months, I was, again, part of a swimming team, where I could develop relationships based on a shared passion. I had missed swimming, but I first thought that it would be hard to train and work in consulting at the same time. Then it occurred to me that without giving it a try, I would never know, and I felt deep in my heart that I needed and wanted swimming. So, I joined a master's team and continued to attend training at least twice a week. The training sessions were enough to sustain my general endurance, and I kept attending national and international championships and winning medals.

WAS IT DIFFICULT TO CONTINUE SWIMMING DESPITE A HARD-CORE CONSULTING JOB?

It would be a lie if I said it was easy to continue swimming. It was hard to keep the pace, to keep the motivation for training and, of course, to find the time. But what is easy in life? Should everything be a piece of cake? Of course, it was difficult. The challenge is how to realize our dreams or follow our passions despite difficulties.

For me, it was a matter of prioritization, managing my time, and keeping my determination and dedication. Of course, it required many sacrifices and discipline. When friends were asking to go out, I needed to think twice and mostly refuse because I knew that I had limited time for sleep before the next early morning training and needed to stay fit and for both my work and swimming.

I followed the following maxim:

IF YOU REALLY WANT AND NEED SOMETHING - YOU GET IT.

Think about your passion. About what makes you happy or energized. If you want to keep following your hobbies, you can do it no matter how busy you are. I am speaking from my experience and observations.

From my business environment, I know some people at the highest levels, such as CEOs and CFOs, who are still swimming or following their hobbies such as golf, running, or attending a half ironman and even winning races.

I can't forget the comment from my first boss: "If you want to be in the consulting business, you need to stop swimming. You can't do both, especially when you want to grow from consultant level to a manager's position and push your career track."

Today, I am a manager in an even bigger and more competitive company, one of the best consulting companies in the world, one of the Big Four, and I am still swimming.

Don't limit your thoughts and behaviors based on others' comments. Even if they are trusted and respected people in your life, like your mother, your boss, or your best friend. You know your limits, your passion, and even if you feel your limits, don't be afraid to push them. You will see what you are capable of.

YOU NEED TO FOLLOW YOUR PASSION AND JUST DO IT FOR YOURSELF.

We can't live life for others. We need to know what makes us happy and gives us the energy to perform for our work or be always available for people who need us, such as our family members. Of course, it's important to be present for others, but you also need to take time for yourself. Don't forget yourself in this busy world. The more you feel in balance, in peace with yourself and strong, the more you can give something to others and share your energy. Be aware of your own energy source and keep that source.

The source of my motivation, of my energy, was swimming. I knew that. I knew what helped me stay fit, happy, and energized. That's why I continue with all the training at least three times a week and the races. This vitality has helped me to sustain my performance in my job and my energy in my private life.

SUMMARY

1. **Nothing is impossible! If you really want something and work for it!**

2. **If you really want and need something - you get it.**

3. **You need to follow your passion and just do it for yourself.**

4. **You are able to manage your hobbies and your hard work at the same time.** It is a question of prioritization, managing your time, and keeping your determination and dedication for everything that you do.

5. **Don't limit your thoughts and your behaviors based on others' comments.** Even if they are trusted and respected people in your life, like your mother, your boss, or your best friend. Everybody has their own thought process, and it is kind of biased.

6. **You know your limits, your passion, and even if you feel your limits, don't be afraid to push them.** You will see and feel what you are capable of.

7

Long-distance swimming was in my blood - 24 hours swimming in Stuttgart

"Life doesn't get easier or more forgiving, we get stronger and more resilient. "

Steve Maraboli, *Life, the Truth, and Being Free*

Every year, pools across Germany host a public 24-hour swim. *Deutscher Schwimmverband (DSV)*, the national German swimming organization, organizes the event in different regions. Originally, the event was held in 1985 to raise interest in the sport and showcase Germany's public pool facilities. Now, it has evolved into a fitness and health extravaganza, open for all to participate by swimming the most laps they can within the 24-hour allotted time. When you register for the swim, you receive a "counting card." It is a little bit old-fashioned, but I like the idea that you cannot see who is in the first place digitally. It makes the game more interesting and pushes you to challenge your limits and try to do your best distance within 24 hours. You give your card to the counter for the lane in which you plan to swim.

The counter will count the laps you swim. When you leave the pool to take a break, to sleep, or go home for a while, you return your card to a file. From there, you retrieve it, give it to a counter again, and continue swimming. When you decide you are done swimming, you submit the card to be counted in the final results.

My lucky number is three. You always need a strategy to handle the challenge in your mind. In this case, I divided my challenge into three. This meant I was in the water three times with a rest between each session. For me, dividing the distance into three parts was helpful. The first part is the first one, so it is easy. The second one is the middle one, and then the third one is the last one. So, it is easier for me to motivate my brain to continue in three steps.

The first year, I started with 33 kilometers. This distance was my limit. I was in the water three times and swam 10 to 12 kilometers each time.

The second year, I decided to swim 3 kilometers more than the previous year, so I aimed to swim 36 kilometers in total. For each time I was in the water, I swam 1 kilometer more and completed the 36 kilometers to break my own record. The next year, I decided to swim an additional 3 kilometers. So I was aiming for a total of 39 kilometers. All went well, and I was in the top three amongst all swimmers. You can't believe how exhausted but happy I felt after that 24-hour swim. It was like a journey, where I found myself in a different dimension, strengthening and testing my resilience, getting stronger and stronger with each kilometer, in the end, beating my previous achievement.

WHERE IS THE LIMIT? WHEN DO YOU SAY STOP TO YOURSELF? WHEN IS IT ENOUGH?

After all those swims, I thought: "Where is the limit?" When will I say it is enough and it is OK? Isn't it like in normal life? You achieve something, and you always want more and more. You compare yourself to others, and of course, there are always better, richer, more successful, more popular, faster, or more beautiful people in the world. For most people, behind "wanting more and more" is the need for happiness. We think that we can be happy if we get more. We think that we will be fulfilled if we achieve more. And if we are the best, then we are happy forever. Is it really like this?

The danger is that what you achieve will never be enough, and you will never feel satisfied with yourself or with what you achieved because you always expect more and more. What is the limit? I was aware of this syndrome and decided that I would be happy and proud of myself if I could beat the marathon distance. That would be my self-record and my limit, where I could stop and say that I achieved something really great in my self-transformation journey.

So, I targeted to swim more than 42.2 kilometers. It was, for me, the limit, my personal goal, my record of myself, and I had the feeling that it would be my highest point in this kind of 24-hour race.

I had already moved to Frankfurt for a new consulting job, where I was working in talent management and psychometric testing. I asked one of my best friends in Stuttgart to stay at her house to join this race. I drove to Stuttgart and started the race at 3 pm. I divided the distance into three parts again. I started to swim and wanted to cover as much distance as I could before midnight. I swam 15 kilometers, with just some toilet and drink breaks. I had some cramps, and it became cold. I swam for approximately 5 hours. I had prepared energy gels, energy bars, and water. After 15 kilometers, I got out and had a break for two hours. I ate my energy bar and a banana and tried to warm myself up. I concentrated for the next round. Each counting card had 15 kilometers, so I went to the desk and asked for another card. They were surprised. I was sure I would swim at least 15 more kilometers.

After the two-hour break, I went into the water again, and I immediately felt cold. My body was already exhausted after 15 kilometers. It was 10 pm. Some swimmers went, others stayed, others prepared camping places to sleep and rest directly by the pool. My body was getting tired, my arms becoming less powerful, and I felt the burn in my shoulders.

I knew that if I could swim as long as I could before the 12-hour mark, then I would be motivated to swim the rest and achieve my goal.

I swam until 3 am. In every previous 24-hour swim, I had gone home and slept for a few hours. I wanted to do the same, but this time, the duration of the break was really limited compared to my previous swims. After 30 kilometers, my arms were burning. Every time I moved my arm, I felt the pain. My nose started to bleed. I couldn't move my arm up and down. It was so painful. I went and took a hot shower, dried my hair, and went to my friend's place. With my arm, even driving was a challenge. When I arrived at her place, I saw that she had prepared pasta for me, and in the guest bed, there were three warm bottle bags ready. I was so happy to see her support, but at the same time, I was at the end of my nerve and my physical capabilities. I felt so tired and powerless and asked myself how I would be able to wake up again and swim another 12 kilometers. I felt the pain in all the cells in my body. I took some aspirin in the hope that I would feel less pain and be able to sleep. After 4 hours, the alarm rang. I felt exhausted. We had a WhatsApp group for our swim team. I decided to write there to find someone who could swim with me and motivate me. I really needed some external motivation. The internal symptoms, both physical and mental, were dominating my willingness to continue. I asked myself why I was doing this. It was so painful. I constantly asked myself this question. I couldn't remember the answer. Or was the answer just my willingness to achieve the goal that I had set for myself? The focus, the willingness to beat myself, my mind. While I had those thoughts and was still in bed, I received an answer in the WhatsApp group. A good friend of mine, Frank, who is a sports teacher, answered my request and said that he would come to the pool and swim with me.

I did not feel alone anymore, and this motivated me, giving me at least a push to wake up, prepare myself, and drive to the pool.

We met at the entrance, got prepared, and started swimming together. After 3 kilometers, Frank said that he would get out. I felt grateful that he at least gave me the power to swim the first kilometer. I hoped to meet some other team members in the pool and see other familiar faces. One other team member came and just swam 1 kilometer. At least, I had something to focus on, to put my attention to, for 20 minutes. It was a good feeling to know I wasn't alone with all other competitors in the pool. A team member is always encouraging in the same lap.

In this kind of long-distance swim, you always need to find something that keeps your mind busy or gives you support indirectly, especially when you are swimming in a pool. I did all these laps in a 50-meter Olympic pool. Unlike running, cycling, or even open water swimming, where the scenery changes and the pursuit of the destination keep you occupied, swimming laps doesn't have built-in entertainment. Besides the pain in your body, the boredom is overwhelming and also painful.

I had cramps again. I got out for a short toilet break and was concerned about my arms. My shoulders burned, and I had difficulty moving my arms. I saw a trainer and asked him a straightforward question: "My pain is still continuing, especially in my arms. Would I have a long-term negative consequence like an injury in my shoulders and arms?" The trainer said: "No, don't worry. It will be painful for now because your lactic acid is now all in your arms, but it has no long-term bad consequences." I trusted his argument because he told me just what I wanted to hear. I wanted to protect myself, my body, but I was so focused on my goal and just wanted to complete my targeted distance despite the pain. After all those hours, I had lost the feeling of time. I had swum 16 hours of the past 22 hours, and I was in a flow. The last two hours, I felt like I was drunk. It was a more intense feeling. It was an intense flow moment, where I lost the feeling of pain, time, and everything around me. Just myself and my focus to finish. The last kilometers. I started to count the meters. I counted every 100 meters and regularly checked with the observers, who were counting my laps, to ensure that they counted my distance right. I tried to stay focused and not lose my mind. How could my body continue despite the pain and boredom? This was exactly the positive psychology of the flow moment.

THE PSYCHOLOGY OF FLOW HELPS YOU TO ACHIEVE YOUR GOALS DESPITE PAIN.

What exactly is flow? My attention during the swim was focused on the movements of my body, the power of my muscles, the force of my lungs, and the feel of the water on my skin. I literally lived in the moment, utterly absorbed in the present activity. Time seemed to fly away. I was tired, but I barely noticed.

According to positive psychologist, Mihály Csíkszentmihályi, what I was experiencing in that moment was known as flow, a state of complete immersion in an activity. He describes the mental state of flow as "being completely involved in an activity for its own sake. The ego falls away. Time flies. Every action, movement, and thought follows inevitably from the previous one, like playing jazz. Your whole being is involved, and you're using your skills to the utmost."

Flow experiences can occur in different ways for different people. Some might experience flow while engaging in a sport, like in my example, such as skiing, tennis, soccer, swimming, or running. Others might have such an experience while engaged in an activity such as painting, drawing, or writing. These moments of flow often occur when you are engaged in an activity that you enjoy and in which you are accomplished.

This state of mind helped me to achieve my goal. I couldn't use my arms properly in the last meters and started utilizing just my feet to move on. I swam until 2.55 pm, 5 minutes before the race stopped. I gave my card to the observers and had a warm shower. I had swum 42.2 kilometers in the past 24 hours, and I had been in the water for a total of 17 hours. What a day?! What a flow experience!

THE FLOW EXPERIENCE - HOW DID IT FEEL FOR ME EXACTLY?

According to Csíkszentmihályi,[1] there are ten factors that accompany the experience of flow. While many of these components may be present, it is not necessary to experience *all* of them for flow to occur:

1. **Clear goals that, while challenging, are still attainable**
   Challenging and realistic goals give you the motivation to put your effort toward it to reach your goal. If it's too easy, it doesn't attract you, if it's too hard, you feel distanced, but if you know your capabilities and which further step you can and will take, then you are unstoppable.

2. **Strong concentration and focused attention**
   It's not easy to focus and keep the concentration, especially in our digital world, where we receive different push messages from different sources all the time, such as our watches, mobile phones, laptops. The more you focus on one thing, the more you enjoy the moment and can use your fullest potential.

1 *(Mindfulness For Dummies - Page 80, Shamash Alidina – 2014).*

3. **The activity is intrinsically rewarding**
   Our intrinsic motivation is the most powerful driver compared to external rewards. The feeling of fulfillment is unpayable. The more we feel success, the more we feel intrinsic rewards and positive feelings.

4. **Feelings of serenity; a loss of feelings of self-consciousness**
   The focus of the moment, like in a meditative state, in what you are self-aware and feel your inner depth.

5. **Timelessness; a distorted sense of time; feeling so focused on the present that you lose track of time passing**
   The more you can focus on the moment and follow your passion, the more you lose the feeling of time. Because time is not important at this moment, you feel just the moment, enjoy what you are doing, and forget everything else in your environment.

6. **Immediate feedback**
   Especially in sports, you receive immediate feedback. You can compare yourself directly with your own previous performance and with your competitors and know about your performance.

7. **Knowing that the task is doable; a balance between skill level and the challenge presented**
   The balance between having a challenging goal and the belief that you can do it with your capabilities gives you the further power and motivation to continue.

8. **Feelings of personal control over the situation and the outcome**
   Even if you feel pain and are sometimes overwhelmed in the situation, the belief in yourself and your own power still gives you the capability to take control over the challenging situation and the results.

9. **Lack of awareness of physical needs**
   In challenging situations, such as sports or business, when you are under time pressure, you feel your body symptoms less and have the motivation and adrenalin to focus on your goal achievement. You partially ignore your symptoms to maximize your performance.

10. **Complete focus on the activity itself**
    When you are clearly focused on what you are doing, you forget yourself and concentrate on the activity itself.

I checked all those factors during my swim, so I can say that I had a flow experience. I had a clear goal, was focused and concentrated. I felt intrinsically rewarded. Nobody forced me to continue my swim and do longer distances. I didn't earn money at the end; I didn't become famous from my achievement. It was just for me to prove to myself what I was capable of and explore my limits, both physically and mentally. I felt that, in some way, I lost my consciousness and sense of time. I tried to control my mind, my emotions, and paid less attention to the needs of my body and pain.

After my hot shower, I came back and started waiting for the results. It was a surprise for all of us, as nobody knew their rank. The awards ceremony started. I was so nervous and curious about the results. They started with the men. The third man swam 39 kilometers, the second 42 kilometers, and the first one 45 kilometers. Afterward, they continued with the women. The third woman swam 38 kilometers. The second one 41 kilometers. And I became the first woman in the overall category with 42.4 kilometers. I was so happy!! My team members hugged me, and I got my cup. I was so happy because I had beaten myself, I explored my own limits, I broke my own record. I became the first woman and second overall, including men.

I felt my adrenalin level and happiness hormones combined with my tiredness. I felt fulfilled and happy with myself. This achievement was enough for me. I didn't think about another 24-hour race. That was my last one. I knew where to push myself, but also where to say it was enough and stop. There is no limit, and you can always go further and further. But this challenge was enough for me. I pushed my limits and saw how far I could go. That satisfied me and made me believe more in myself and my strengths. I was so grateful for this flow experience. It gave me so much, and I learned to have more endurance, patience, resilience, and focus with this experience.

Never give up, always follow your flow, continue, do what helps you in this journey, and beat yourself. Every time you beat yourself, you are getting stronger, learning new things, and figuring out a new version of yourself – just like a piece of magic!

SUMMARY

1. **Reflect when's the best time to stop.** When you achieve something, you tend to always want more and more. You compare yourself to others, and of course, there are always better, richer, more successful, more popular, faster, or more beautiful people in the world. For most people, behind "wanting more and more" is the need for happiness. We think that we can be happy if we get more. We think that we will be fulfilled if we achieve more. And if we are the best, then we are happy forever. Know your limits and stop yourself when you reach the right level. Your body, mind, and soul will tell you when you need to stop.

2. **The Psychology of Flow helps you to achieve your goals despite pain**. Flow experiences can occur in different ways for different people. Some might experience flow while engaging in a sport, like in my example, such as skiing, tennis, soccer, swimming, or running. Others might have such an experience while engaged in an activity such as painting, drawing, working, or writing. These moments of flow often occur when you are engaged in an activity that you enjoy and in which you are accomplished.

3. **Never give up, always follow your flow.** Continue, do what helps you in this journey, and beat yourself. Every time you beat yourself, you are getting stronger, learning new things, and figuring out a new version of yourself – just like a piece of magic!

8

How swimming shaped my personality, my private and business life

Swimming shaped my personality. Through my competitive swimming journey, I learned many new dimensions and transformed my natural potential into strengths that have helped me in my entire school life, and are still helping me in my corporate and private life.

1. **Endurance:**
   First of all, I have the **endurance** to do things, even if I am getting tired. The same in sports or corporate life. The real competition, or the real game, starts when you feel tired. The strong one wins at the end of the game. Getting tired doing things is completely normal; we are all human beings. The question is how you deal with this feeling and push your limits despite hurdles. I learned to overcome the hurdles and push my limits and expand my inner strength both physically and mentally. No matter how tired you are, there is always a hidden power in you to continue even more strongly in the last meters of your challenge.

2. **Resilience:**
Second, I became more **resilient** because I have learned not only to win but also to lose and deal with being less successful. I have become a fighter. I fight against my limits and try to be better without giving up. The more I have worked hard and become better, the more I have gained confidence in all areas of my life. Small things do not affect me because I know the pain and how to deal with it. The more I feel pain, and overcome it, the more I learn to control my mind and body and try to see an opportunity in the situation. The more I control my mind and body, the more I become resilient. Most of the time, it's not just about your past experiences or your physical capabilities. It is about your mind. Your thoughts shape your performance. Your strongest asset is your mind and mental health, which define your resilience.

3. **Collaboration – Teamwork:**
Third, many people think that swimming is an individual sport, but with swimming, I have also learned **collaboration**, training together, supporting each other, even if you are competitors. Your success, even in an individual sport, is still the result of an overall ecosystem. Without this ecosystem, you can't be successful. My family, my trainer, and my friends all supported me to the fullest mentally. You always need supporters in life and also people who challenge you and who give you feedback. Without the feedback of my trainers, I wouldn't have had the perfect technique for both pool and open water swimming. Without the mental challenge of my mom, I wouldn't have had the courage to keep going, and without the support of my friends, I wouldn't have felt part of a team, belonging to something bigger. My friends, family, colleagues, trainer, and coaches contributed to my achievements, and I enjoyed the synergy effects. For example, my swimmer friends swam with me, pushed me as pacemakers, and, at the same time, my friends and family supported me mentally and psychologically.

4. **Mind and Body Control:**
   Swimming also taught me to **know and control my mind and body** and use my external resources to the fullest to maximize my success. Without knowing your body and thought process, you can't be successful and lead others, especially in business, and you can't cultivate your strengths and the potential of others. In every training and challenging race, I experienced my body and my thought process. I learned how to maximize my efficiency and use external or internal sources. In the past, before every championship, I felt so nervous that I would get ill a few days before the race. I usually even had a fever before a big race. I was mentally so nervous that my body got sick. With time, I got to know my strengths, and I also know where I need external support to maximize my success and cultivate my potential. Now, I am not getting ill before a race and can control my nervousness and try to use these emotions to maximize my success and turn it into concentration, willingness to succeed, and focus.

5. **Time Management & Planning:**
   Many people still can't believe that I can keep my swim performance in races and train regularly as well as my busy consulting job. But you can do many things if you have the right **time management** and if you are following the right priorities in a disciplined way. Time management requires discipline and **efficiency**. Through swimming, I learned to be efficient, to have a sense and feeling of time, especially in sprint races, every second, even millisecond matters. I know the importance of time and distribute my hours per day and the days per week, based on my priorities. I learned to be disciplined, to follow my schedule strictly; otherwise, the planned schedule is not possible to follow. There are always distractions in life. Even our inner voices distract us and hold us from doing things, as we just want to sit and do nothing. At this point, the inner discipline and time management help you to go forward despite hurdles. And of course, you also need to

be flexible in life. I learned to set buffer and regeneration zones to feel relaxed and less under pressure - having time for friends or just enjoying doing nothing.

6. **Growth mindset & Achievement Orientation:**
   In every training session, I want to be better and beat my own best time. I want to **achieve** better results all the time. That's the main aim of my training. I want to **improve** my technique, my mindset, my time, and my endurance. That's the goal of training. I don't compete primarily with others; I compete with myself. My training efforts give me a growth mindset, with the aim to be better. I know what I could do in the past, but I don't know what I am capable of in the future. Based on the goals, I try to improve personally, break my own limits, and demonstrate a growth mindset, which help me in my corporate life as well.

SUMMARY

Sports help you both in your corporate and private life. By doing sport, you learn new dimensions in your life. Based on my experiences, it strengthens your mind and body and also your potential in the following areas:

- ▶ Endurance
- ▶ Resilience
- ▶ Collaboration – Teamwork
- ▶ Mind and body control
- ▶ Time management and planning
- ▶ Growth mindset and achievement orientation

9

Cold water – Out of comfort zone

COLD WATER CHANGED MY LIFE. IT TRANSFORMED MY BODY AND BRAIN. IT HELPED ME TO RE-PROGRAM MY CURRENT MENTAL SYSTEM.

Cold water was always my out of comfort zone. My brain and body have negative associations with cold water.

In our lives, we have conscious or subconscious inner blocks, negative associations we are not even aware of. Something in our childhood may have affected us. Maybe, we had a sad experience, or our parents scared us unconsciously from something. It is important to reflect on the origin of those blocks or fears, to face them, and lead ourselves to a better, more powerful direction without letting our fears or bad associations control us.

SO, WHERE DID I GET THOSE NEGATIVE ASSOCIATIONS WITH COLD WATER?

When I was fourteen, I joined the national open water swim trials, which took place in beautiful Marmaris on the Aegean coast. The distance was 10 kilometers. At that time, open water swimming races were quite new in Turkey. We were just three women and around ten men who were chosen to try for the national team.

This meant that if I could complete the 10 kilometers, even if I were the slowest woman, I would automatically be chosen for the national team and could take part in international open water swim races. To be in an international team and represent my country had always been my dream. I was so near to making my dream come true.

The racing day came. There was a 2.5-kilometer track, and we needed to swim four rounds. The observers, the security crew, and the swimmers were ready. After the start sign, we jumped into the water. Oh my god, I remember the first moment I felt the water. It was literally freezing. I couldn't breathe for a few seconds. I felt my heartbeat in my brain. It was fast and strong. I tried to adapt to the cold water. My body and my brain were surprised; they didn't expect this kind of cold water. Normally, wetsuits would be required if the water temperature was below 18 degrees. The water at that time was for sure below 18. After the first round, I saw some swimmers go out. They couldn't handle the cold. I checked the female swimmers. One was still in the water in front of me. She was doing well with her pace and strokes. I was OK and continued to the second round. After the second round, I saw that the rest of the swimmers had gone out as well. In the third round, just she and I remained in the water. I felt the cold in all my cells. I didn't feel well. I had a feeling that I was literally losing my consciousness. I missed the race buoy and tried to find the right track again. My mind was telling me: You need to swim these 10 kilometers no matter your pace or strokes. Just finish it. When you finish, you will be in the national team. Just continue. Just continue, don't give up. Don't think of giving up. She is still in front of you. You are behind her, and it is OK. You will finish the 10 kilometers no matter how you feel. When I had those thoughts and tried to continue my swim, the observers in the boat came to me and asked if I felt OK. I said: "Yes, all good!" That was the maximum level of my speaking ability. I literally started to shake. My whole body and my teeth were shaking. I continued to swim and ignored their further comments because the more I stayed, the more I would feel the cold and lose control of my body. I continued, but without knowing where I was. I just swam and told myself: "You can't give up! You need to continue!" After 10 minutes, the boat with the observers came to me again. They stopped me and said that I didn't look good, and I needed to get out. Everybody was out, and I needed to get out. I was annoyed and so focused on my goal, I didn't accept their verdict and continued to swim. I can't remember what I said or what I did. I only remember that I continued to swim. I was too focused on the result. I didn't feel the journey anymore. I ignored my body, my symptoms, and the cold. My focus was just on the result; I wasn't even aware that I wasn't going in the right direction.

TUNNEL VISION CAN BE DANGEROUS

Was it too much focus or something else? Maybe, I was just too focused. Or maybe, I just did not want to fail? Or I had a tunnel vision, which means that the edges of your vision are lost, and only the central focus remains as if you are looking through a tunnel. It is a lack of perspective caused by an intense focus on one object, leading to the neglect of surroundings and responsibilities, or being closed off to other viewpoints. I had that kind of tunnel vision when I studied and worked.

A few minutes later, a second, bigger boat approached me. I checked the people in the boat. It was hard to see because of my fogged goggles. They stopped me again. This time, I saw the chief referee. He spoke to me in a serious manner and said that I had to come out. Again, I refused and said that I wanted to continue, but this time, I was finding it too difficult to speak. My mind felt confused, and my body felt weak. I felt pressure in my arms. He pulled me out of the water. I had been in the water for 2 ½ hours, not realizing that I had been in for so long. I was in a trance, and the only thing I said was: "Why have you stopped me, I wanted to continue swimming, I wanted to complete the 10 kilometers distance!" I blamed them for pulling me out.

I can't remember what happened afterward. I found myself in an ambulance, or was it a hospital? What I knew was that I felt the warm heating blanket on my wet skin and opened my eyes. One nurse asked me how I felt. I asked her: "What happened to me?" She said: "You had hypothermia." I didn't want to accept it and asked again exactly what had happened to me. She answered: "You lost consciousness; your body temperature was below 35.0 °C (95.0 °F)." In mild hypothermia, there is shivering and mental confusion. In moderate hypothermia, shivering stops and confusion increases. The chief referee said that I had lost my direction in the water, couldn't speak properly, and was shivering. That meant I had moderate hypothermia, and that's why they needed to warm up my body. I thanked him and closed my eyes again. I was too exhausted to say anything and tried to accept that I couldn't complete the distance. I couldn't believe that I had hypothermia and had swum in this cold water for 2.5 hours. But now, it makes sense. I was in another world, and if they hadn't have pulled me out of the water, I might have died. The chief referee and his team had saved my life. I was grateful and happy that I had survived. Ten years later, I saw him in the Arena Aquamasters swimming cup, and we hugged each other with tears in our eyes. We became so emotional. He said that he had saved my life, and I felt grateful again. I was so happy to see him after so many years.

After this experience, you can imagine that cold water was a taboo for me. I associated cold water with danger, illness, and being out of my comfort zone.

BUT WHY DID I START WITH COLD WATER IMMERSIONS?

My dream was always to swim the English Channel. But I knew that the English Channel is freezing cold, and I needed to gain weight and train hard and long to deal with the cold water. So, I parked this dream and continued with my consulting and "normal" swimming life.

After ten years, my cousin, living in Datça, the place where I had started open water swimming, said that he had met someone who was looking for a swimming partner to swim from the Greek island Symi to the Turkish coast at Datça. I was, of course, more than happy to meet this person. His name was Emre Deliveli. He was an economist who did his Ph.D. at Harvard University and was now living in Marmaris, managing his family business. After we met each other, we started to plan the swim. For him, it was a big challenge because he had started swimming less than a year previously when he was 40 years old and had never swum long distances. He wanted to explore his limits with an experienced swimmer. In this case, it was me.

It was hard to find an escort boat. Finally, Emre arranged a boat, but the captain declined to take us the day before the swim. He later admitted that he first thought we were refugees trying to escape to Greece. When I showed him my German passport, he felt relieved. We didn't get any formal approval from the Greeks, or for that matter, the Turkish coast guard, either. Everything about this swim felt risky, and my family members wanted to stop me from doing it. We should have traveled with the Greek police during our swim in the Greek waters, and we didn't know the route properly, and we didn't know each other as well. My swim buddy and I could end up getting arrested by the Greek coast guard.

I like risks. I loved the idea of trying this risky route and accomplishing another challenge. I feel attracted to these kinds of experiences. I felt a sense of both respect and fear of the unknown.

When the day came, Emre, my mum, the captain, and I started in the early morning and went toward the Greek island of Symi. Since we had not applied for a permit, we didn't go all the way into the harbor and started from outside Symi. When we jumped into the water, my mother was in a panic. She was afraid that something bad would happen in the water. The water temperature was OK, the water felt nice. We started to swim. The captain tried to follow our pace and the right route to guide us. We had several drinking breaks. It felt so exciting to swim in the middle of the Aegean Sea, and when we checked left and right, we saw nothing. There was only the endless sea. I could feel nature to the fullest. My mum and the captain motivated us and checked our wellbeing. After 13 kilometers, we saw the coast. It was an amazing feeling to see it and realize that we had done it!

Despite our different backgrounds and paces, we'd managed to swim in harmony, supporting each other mentally in the water, and we completed the route by ourselves. We used this swim to collect donations for the victims of the fires in Greece, which had resulted in deaths and loss of property shortly before our swim. I was so happy to have completed the route, while at the same time, supporting people in need.

After the swim, we celebrated with mojitos and started to discuss future swim plans. That's what we naturally do as human beings, right? When we achieve our goals, our brains have difficulty relaxing and enjoying the moment, starting instead to think about the next chapters.

I told Emre about my English Channel dream. I had always wanted to swim the English Channel. I have so much respect for people who have done it, and it's the Mount Everest of swimming. I knew that a solo swim, in which you swim the whole distance alone without touching the support boat, would be tough because of the cold water, and given the limited time I have in my busy consulting work to train. But I could imagine doing a relay swim, which means that you swim as part of a team and split the route. Each swimmer enters the water for one hour in a predetermined order, and depending on the size of the team, each would be swimming three or four times. That seemed feasible to me. The only hurdle was to find teammates, whom you could trust and go through this journey together. I had a feeling that I had found at least one person; he was sitting in front of me.

A few weeks later, I went back to Germany to my normal consulting life. One day, the phone rang after work. Emre was calling me to say that he had found the best person to coach us for our English Channel swim, someone who had swum the English Channel several times and also coached people who wanted to do the same. His name was Kamil Resa Alsaran - little did I know at the time that he would play such an important role in my cold water journey. He said that Kamil would organize a slot for us and that he could also find two teammates. With his support, we could get the slot for this year, as there is usually a two-year waiting list!

I was shocked and amazed at the same time. My dream would come true. I wouldn't swim solo, but at least I could do a relay swim in the English Channel in freezing water and still test my limits in a unique and natural environment with a team, which would give me a more secure feeling.

We started to plan the date and speak with possible team members. I cannot understate the importance of the team members. You are paying so much money for the swim, organizing everything, but if one team member fails during the swim, then your whole swim would be canceled. That means trust, collaboration, transparency, equal preparation, and training are key.

I had the feeling that now was the right time to plan this relay. I had the feeling that I had at least found the right swim partner to plan further. Besides organizational and financial matters, the most important part waited for us - getting used to cold water out of our comfort zone!

COLD IMMERSIONS - OUT OF OUR COMFORT ZONE

Swimming in cold water is a big challenge for all of us. There are different definitions of cold water. Most organizations define cold water as under 17 degrees Celsius. But most people feel cold under 21 degrees. The temperature of a swimming pool is, on average, 27 degrees. You can imagine how water below 17 degrees feels. Our body is not used to the cold. When you experience cold, your body responds in several noticeable ways. Your blood vessels constrict—a process called vasoconstriction—taking blood away from your extremities and keeping it near your core. And you shiver, meaning certain muscles start shaking to produce heat. But shivering also triggers the release of a hormone called irisin, which jump-starts a lesser-known cold response: the activation and buildup of brown fat.

THE ROLE OF BROWN FAT IN COLD WATER

The brown fat, which protects us from cold, does not normally exist in adults. We have those brown fat cells only when we are babies. Brown fat is different from the white fat we might think of when discussing diet or weight loss. White fat lines our skin and muscles, cushioning our organs and bones. But brown fat appears only in specific areas around the neck, spine, aorta, and kidneys. It builds up in clumps around major blood vessels, warming the blood as it passes through the body. "If vasoconstriction is closing the window, brown fat is turning on the heater," says Yossi Rathner, a physiologist at the University of Melbourne.

But the effect only lasts for as long as we need it. When the temperature warms up, brown fat fades away. "If we are not exposed to the cold, the brown fat will atrophy," says Barbara Cannon, a physiologist at Stockholm University. "There may be a few stem cells left in the area for later regeneration, but it will nearly disappear," Cannon says.

Even a one-month tropical vacation is enough to deplete one's brown fat reserves, Celi says, creating that "extra cold" sensation a traveler might feel upon returning to a cold climate.

You could say brown fat is winter's undercover hero, dropping in when we need it most, and disappearing once the job is done. That's why continuous cold-water training for the body is key to keeping the brown fat in the body and activating the inner heating system.

In this chapter, I will share my journey with you, how I got used to cold water, how I felt, and how I trained day by day, month by month for ten months, and how I transformed my body and mind.

OUT OF THE COMFORT ZONE DAY 1 – 10TH NOVEMBER 2018

I hated cold water and enjoyed hot showers and hot water in spas. But it was now time to unlock my inner barriers and fears and start to love cold water. Did I really say love? Could I really love cold water? I honestly didn't know. I knew it would be a challenge for me. It was out of my comfort area. In the English Channel, the water temperature would be around 15-16 degrees. For me, that is freezing.

My swim partner, good friend, and motivator, Emre, came from Turkey to Germany at the end of October, and we went to Raunheimer Waldsee Lake, where I had swum many times before, but always in the summer. The Baggersee in Raunheim is surrounded by forest all around, which makes it particularly beautiful. You can swim in the summer from a large, sandy beach. For more action on the water, there is also a water ski system. There is always something going on at Raunheimer, and a trip is worthwhile. The beach is open from mid-May to mid-September. In October, the lake was closed, of course, and swimming was not allowed. So what did we do? Despite the circumstances, we still went into the water and explained the situation to the team on site. We swam in 14.9 degrees water for 40 minutes! It was the first time that I'd swam in such cold water. Emre motivated me with his presence, and I thought I needed to swim with him because that was the reason he had come all the way from Turkey. It's so important to believe and motivate each other in life. There are sparring partners in life with whom you can share the journey. So, in the end, what happened? We are still alive and healthy! Of course, we had the shakes for 30 minutes (after a freezing swim session, this is quite normal), but in the end, we were proud and felt alive!

OUT OF COMFORT ZONE DAY 2 – 11TH NOVEMBER 2018

Another day of cold-water immersion. I swam in the same lake in 13 degrees of cold water for 33 minutes. It was getting colder day by day. My mind was focused, and before I went into the water, I tried to control my breathing. My body felt the pain; it was hard. I couldn't breathe at the beginning but was happy to do it again. After the first experience, it was easier to concentrate and go into the water. I felt that my inner barriers had a lower effect, and my confidence was higher than the first time. That's life, isn't it? We always have some fears, some barriers, but the art is to overcome them. Happy to have had my first experience. Believe in yourself, face your fears, and go the extra mile step by step. Even if it feels hard, even if you feel sad or not strong enough. It's time to start to extend your limits and explore your potential!

WE ARE STRONGER THAN WE THINK! DAY 3 – 14TH NOVEMBER 2018

The 14th of November was the third time that I swam. It was getting colder still, and each time I was going to the lake, it was a new challenge, a new feeling of coldness. Winter had arrived. No sun and a windy day. It was getting harder to step into this freezing water every time. I was nervous and even a little afraid. A new experience meant a new version of handling the challenge and a new version of myself. I started to google videos about cold water training. I found out about the Wim Hof breathing technique to have more control of my body and have more confidence. I did some meditation to focus better and get mentally prepared for the cold water. I prepared myself mentally and physically with breathing techniques. When I was there and measured the water temperature, I thought, "Oh my God?! Can I really do this?" It was 12.5 degrees. Wouldn't it be too risky for my heart and body? But then I said, "No, I am strong, and I have the control of my body and mind." I took a deep breath and went into the water. I felt the pain first in my feet, and then, when I was completely in the water, I felt it in my head, and it felt as if my body was burning. Each cell of my body was burning. I tried to use the positive saying: "Love this feeling!" There is cold water, and you are feeling this coldness. Love it and continue to swim with controlled breathing. Every three strokes, one breath: one time left, one time right. My eyes were closed at first, but I pushed myself to open them to follow my swim mate, watch the nature behind me, try to keep awake, and handle the coldness with control and positive feelings. After 1 km, I wanted to stop my swim. I felt that I was getting slower; my body tried to keep warm and fought. I swam 500 meters more. I felt so alive and happy. I felt relieved, as well. I had broken my inner barriers and fears again, and now I was sitting in my warm living room, drinking hot tea, and still feeling endorphin hormones. We humans are stronger than we think. Almost everything starts in our mind. Our inner beliefs and thoughts are formed from the outside world. Most of the time, we are influenced by external factors. Many people asked me: "Are you crazy? It's dangerous, don't do that!" But why not? It's always a challenge to follow your passion and go your own way despite others' opinions, without feeling out of balance. There is a nice saying: "I am not afraid to die, I am afraid not to live to the fullest. Follow your passion! You are stronger than you think!" - Wim Hof

OUT OF COMFORT ZONE - DAY 4 – 20TH NOVEMBER 2018

It was getting colder and colder, winter was coming, and today was windy. The air temperature 4 degrees, but the sun was shining. I had the need to go to the lake again and feel the cold water. My body wanted to go out of my comfort zone again and feel a new experience. Each time I went into the water, it was a new temperature and, therefore, a new feeling – a new version of me who was coping with the new challenge. I called my German open water swim buddy, Torsten, who had been swimming with me with a wetsuit. It was cold, even with my jacket. But I wanted to try to swim again without a wetsuit. The few people and coaches in the wakeboard area announced us "officially crazy." We measured the water temperature; it was 10 degrees, 2.5 degrees less than the last time. In this kind of temperature, you can feel even a 0.5-degree difference. I thought, "Oh my God. How can I do this?" I started to concentrate and walked step by step toward the water. When I touched the water, it was really freezing. I had many thoughts, fears in my mind, and tried to control those with constant deep breathing. Breathing in and out, each time deeper and deeper, as I felt the cold water, starting on my feet, then knees, then belly and hands, arms, shoulders, and my face. It was hard to breathe in the cold water. My body was exposed to an extreme condition, and I tried to keep calm and continue to inhale and exhale. In the end, I could swim for 10 minutes. Wow. When I got out, I was happy to have had this experience. I felt alive and proved to myself that many blocks are only in our minds.

We are able to control our bodies with our minds, making our souls happy.

IMAGINE - BELIEVE - ACHIEVE! FIRST ICE SWIM EXPERIENCE, 20TH JANUARY 2019

My first Ice Swim with a wetsuit! What an amazing and challenging experience. That was definitely out of my comfort zone. It was cold outside, about -1 degrees, and I decided to go to the lake with Torsten and Tariq, the swim coach from the Hilton Hotel, where I swim all the time in Frankfurt. The water temperature was about 4 degrees. Many people told me not to do it. But my inner voice wanted to try, even though I was afraid. In fact, my fear motivated me to do it. What an interesting state of mind, right? Two weeks ago, I couldn't imagine that; two days ago, I had asked myself what if I tried? And today was the day. But it's always important to know your limits and have a step-by-step approach. I'm happy to have done it—respect to my swimming friends all over the world who can do this without a wetsuit.

BELIEVE IN YOURSELF- ACHIEVE!

Extended inner border: Cold Water Training Camp at Usedom, Germany

One of my best friends, Kristin, lives in Usedom. We studied together at Bochum Ruhr University and did our business psychology masters. She is now working as a psychologist in a clinic. I use every opportunity to visit her when I swim in the Usedom sea. Her house is just 200 meters away from the beach. Usedom is a Baltic sea island, divided between Germany and Poland since 1945. It is the sunniest region in Germany. This time, I was lucky because the sun was shining, but the water temperature was still only about 7 degrees. It was, for me, the best condition to go out of my comfort zone again and try to extend the duration of my cold water swims. The more I trained, the longer I could stay in the cold water. It was great to see my progress.

Day 1, 23rd November 2019: I started to run early in the morning, and after that, I went directly into the water. It was a real challenge. I had sweated because of the sun, and my body was hot. I felt the temperature difference more than the usual. After 6 minutes, I couldn´t feel my legs or my back. I got out. It was the first time that I was completely alone, with no external motivation or support. It was real mental toughness training, but I felt my limit and got out at the right time. I was afraid because I couldn't feel my legs. My body was completely red, but afterward, I felt energized and fulfilled.

Day 2, 24th November 2019: In the morning, I ran to the Polish side of the island. The distance was around 8 kilometers. It took me about 60 minutes. After the run, I had breakfast with Kristin and her husband, Mike. It is always amazing to eat after an intense training session. Especially after cold water immersion, I allow myself to eat anything I want and have a rest. I had learned from day one that it was not good to swim in the cold water with a sweaty body and a high body temperature. Around lunchtime, I went to the beach, this time with Kristin. She motivated me and said: "Think that the sun is warming your body, and you are in the middle of summer." She is a psychologist, too, and tried to give me mental advice. When I was in the water, I forgot to think about all those hints. I just focused on the swim and didn´t think about other things. I saw her outside as a mental anchor and safety support. She gave me a sign after 10 minutes. I wanted to break my own record and wanted to swim at least 11 minutes in this kind of cold water, which was below 8 degrees Celsius. In the end, I was in for 14 minutes. It felt so great, and I was happy. The more it challenged me, the happier it made me.

Pain is growth.
After pain, there come magical moments of growth, which are the special moments we need to enjoy. Without pain, no gain.

Winter Camp in Turkey, January 2019
After Germany, I went to Turkey during Christmas and did a swimming camp with my swim buddy Emre.

Day 1: Marmaris, Aegean Sea, Water temperature 14 degrees
We swam without a wetsuit for 45 minutes. It was really challenging. We thought that the water temperature was around 17-18, but we were shocked when we saw it was just 14 degrees, which is very unusual for this region at this time of the year. We motivated each other and swam in this freezing water. Afterward, it took me half an hour to get back to normal. The shakes were there again, and after this kind of cold immersion, it is important not to take a hot shower right away. The veins in our body contract in response to the cold and expand when exposed to heat. A hot shower right after a cold water swim is not recommended, as the sudden expansion in the veins may result in fainting. I just couldn't wait and had a hot shower for half an hour.

Day 2: Selimiye, Aegean Sea, Water temperature 17 degrees
After the first day, my body and my mind felt really tired. The cold immersion was tiring for my body. If your body is not used to this kind of cold water, it can be a real pressure. We went to Selimiye to eat something first. It was cold and rainy. It was hard to get the motivation to swim again. We motivated each other. The water felt cold; my body and mind felt exhausted. I forced myself to go in despite my negative thoughts.

After 15 minutes of swimming, I just wanted to get out, sit by the fire, and eat some nice food and drink something hot. I asked Emre about the time, and he said, "15 minutes" in a shivering tone. I thought it was a joke. Only 15 minutes, and I was already freezing. Normally, I like the waves, but this time they felt hard to handle and exhausting. I tried to push myself and watch the beautiful mountains of Selimiye while I breathed left and right every three strokes. In the end, we stayed in the water for 60 minutes. Afterward, I felt completely exhausted. On the other hand, I felt proud. Despite all those negative thoughts and feelings, I managed to control myself and swam for one hour. This showed me that I was capable of more than what my mind was thinking. Sometimes, our mind is playing games with us and searching for comfort. It wants to be in the zone where everything is predictable, easy to handle, less complicated. But if you push yourself and go the extra mile, then extraordinary things happen, and you start to believe in yourself more than ever. You are going to the next level in your inner world. This feeling of stepping out of your comfort zone gives you more power and self-confidence. Not only in the water but also in your life, both professionally and personally. I felt much more relaxed in my hardcore consulting life after those cold water immersions. I felt how my stress level was reduced, and even in challenging times, I managed to calm down quickly by taking a deep breath and activating my solution-focused mindset with more confidence.

Day 3: Datça, Aegean Sea, Water temperature was 17 degrees
On Day 3, we swam at Datça, my favorite place, for 70 minutes. The water was amazing as always, and we swam from one island to another. Those islands, Adaburnu and Tuz, are my favorite islands in Datça. This is the place where I always swam and meditated alone. Just the nature, the sound of the waves, of the birds and me. When I swim there, I feel freedom, being a part of nature, and forgetting everything around me. This time was different because it was the first time that I had swam this route in winter, and my body was tired and more sensitive to the cold. But sharing this challenge with Emre motivated me, giving me the power to not give up and swim at least more than 60 minutes. But it was not easy. I constantly tried to motivate myself, speaking to myself, and pushing my desire to stay in the water. Whenever you feel you want to stop something, don't forget that that is the exact moment you need to convince yourself to keep doing what you are doing. Activate and improve your mental and physical endurance. It's about keeping going despite hurdles and pain.

6 min in 6-degree water in Holland – Nordwjik en Zee
I went for a business trip to Holland on 18th February 2019. We had our new manager training program there right after my promotion to a manager's position. I went with my close colleague, Vivian Aschke. We met each other two days before the conference to have a short holiday in Amsterdam together. We had shared our career journey and worked on projects together for

the past two years, and so it was a great feeling to go together to this manager conference to celebrate our career progress. I loved having my friends around me for my cold-water mission, and thanks to the support of different people in my life, I could continue with those cold immersions no matter where I was. I convinced Vivian to go to the beach in Noordwijk, which is a town in the west of the Netherlands, in the province of South Holland.

It was a windy and cold day. People with warm clothes, gloves, and hats were walking around the beach. They saw me with my swimsuit, and they probably thought: "She is crazy." Maybe I was! I hadn't heard this for the first time. But who cares? I like to test my limits, to go out of my comfort zone, and with each cold immersion, I feel stronger than before. Thankfully, Vivian supported and waited for me with a dry towel. It was so great to share this journey with my friends and colleagues and feel the real support from everyone everywhere. I was so grateful to all my friends who supported me all over the world and shared this journey with me.

SAYING THANK YOU AGAIN AND AGAIN TO ALL THE PEOPLE IN MY LIFE WITH WHOM I COULD EXPERIENCE THESE COLD WATER IMMERSIONS!

---

5 Minutes in 3-degree water in Berlin

For another business trip, I was in Berlin in February 2019. During the weekdays, I managed a digital transformation SAP change management project, where I supported the client to motivate and upskill their employees to deal with the upcoming structural changes. I used this business opportunity to stay in Berlin over a weekend. Despite my tired body and busy week, I wanted to challenge myself again and wanted to stay in the water longer than my previous swims. My friends from Berlin Marcel and Anne motivated me and brought me to a nice lake where I could swim. The lake was called *Gruenewaldsee*, which is in the western *Bezirk Charlottenburg-Wilmersdorf* in Berlin within the *Gruenewald*, which literally translates as "green forest." They waited for me on the shore with a dry towel. When I touched the water, it felt freezing. I tried to control my mind and breath. It was hard to go step by step into the water. I felt I couldn't do it and wanted to go back to my friends. But my inner voice said, "Come on, you are almost in, just do it." I had a fear that something bad would happen- e.g. my heart would stop. I kept breathing and started to swim. It took me one minute to acclimatize, but after that, I felt so great that I could stay 4 more minutes. I felt so strong and happy. So many things start and end in our minds. When I was out, they gave me the towel, and I felt so blessed and lucky to be surrounded in a supportive atmosphere, which warmed me up more than the towel. After the swim, we walked ten minutes to the car, and I concentrated on not having the shakes with active deep breathing and tried to activate my inner fire. If the shakes come, you can't control them, and it takes me around 30 minutes, at least, to return to normal. But breathing and focus helped me to control the shakes after these swims.

3 minutes in 3-degree Icebach with Bikini in Munich, 3rd February 2019

I was again in Munich for business purposes. Munich Business School had invited my colleagues and me as guest lecturers; I regularly gave lectures about change management, talent management, and the future of work. One of my best friends, Theresa Herbig, whom I had met in Stuttgart in the gym, had moved to Munich for a great new career path. Every time I am there, we try to see each other. Theresa also likes to try new things in life and explore the world and herself.

I came to her with a crazy idea that I had heard so many times from friends who had done ice-swimming. For me, it was unbelievable to go this step without a wetsuit. I stayed over the weekend and wanted to swim in Eisbach. The Eisbach (German for "ice brook") is a small, two kilometer-long, manmade river in Munich. It flows through the park known as the *Englischer Garten* and is a side arm of the Isar River. A manmade wave has been created in one section. **Swimming in** the Eisbach is not technically allowed, but as the rule is not stringently enforced; swimmers can be seen, especially on warm summer days

This weekend, I motivated Theresa to go into the freezing water as well. She was crazier than me and said that she would wear her bikini. I accepted the additional challenge. Our friend and former colleague, Andreas, also came with us to observe and protect us as well as wait for us with towels. In this kind of swim, it's always important to have someone who is on the shore to observe. The weather and water temperature were both 3 degrees, and I was in the water for 3 minutes. First, we walked in a little bit. I felt tingling in my foot, and it was a real pain. When my full body was in the water, I felt needles throughout my body. My heartbeat was fast, and I couldn't breathe for a few seconds. I tried to swim for two minutes. It was an intense feeling. My body and mind were overwhelmed by the cold. I was afraid because of my body's reaction. These symptoms were new to me, and therefore, it was hard to decide when to stop the cold immersion. The right timing is key. But with this kind of small step, I think everybody is able to explore their limits, go beyond those and achieve individual growth both physically and mentally. I was again grateful for the friendship and support on this journey. It's hard to do this kind of activity alone.

SHARING THE JOURNEY WITH FRIENDS AND FAMILY IS THE MOST BEAUTIFUL THING.

---

10 Minutes Ice Bath Challenge in Frankfurt - The more you have extraordinary goals in your life, the more you are alone in your journey

This kind of journey is not easy because, most of the time, you are alone. Most people hate cold water and don't train toward these kinds of goals, and it's hard to get support from friends.

The more you have extraordinary goals in your life, the more you are alone in your journey. Of course, you have people who support you, but it's harder to find a partner to train or work with you all the time, everywhere. Especially if you are a person who is traveling a lot like me. I didn't always have the opportunity to drive to a lake. Because I was careful, I never swam alone in cold water. It was not always easy to find other "crazy people" who came and swam with me or waited for me on the shore. So, I always tried to be creative in my personal transformation journey. After an ordinary swim in the pool, I decided to stay 10 minutes in the freezing water where you would normally go after a sauna session in Hilton Frankfurt. I asked my good funny friend and dedicated swim buddy, Kristian Schneider, to support me mentally. He came with me and waited for me outside. I managed to stay for 10 minutes. During this time, Kristian asked me some questions to check if I was OK. Kristian is a great coach, mentor, and motivator. I was lucky to have him during this experience. What I learned from this training session was: "Challenge your mind and body in a creative way. Believe in yourself, and you will be surprised what you are capable of!" Let's jump into the cold! What can you do right now to improve your mental toughness? Start now!

ENGLISH CHANNEL QUALIFIER CAMP: 2 HOURS UNDER 15 DEGREES WATER TEMPERATURE IN ACHENSEE, AUSTRIA

Both solo and relay swimmers need to complete a qualifier swim to be able to register for an English Channel swim. A relay swimmer needs to complete a two-hour swim in water at a temperature of 15 degrees Celsius or under (no wetsuit allowed, only swim hat, goggles, and standard swimsuit). A solo swimmer has to complete a six-hour swim under the same conditions.

In order to swim two hours below 15 degrees, I needed to first find water at this temperature. Because spring had come, the weather was becoming warmer day by day, and the lake temperatures in Frankfurt were around 18 degrees. That meant I needed to find a new place where the water was colder.

Many swimmers have difficulty finding places to complete their qualifier swims safely. My swim buddy Emre and I also had difficulties finding a suitable and safe body of cold water. He came from Turkey to swim in the cold water.

We drove to Tegernsee, a lake near Munich. Tegernsee is a beautiful spa town, surrounded by an alpine landscape in Upper Bavaria, where the economy is mainly based on tourism. When I arrived and checked the water, it was 19 degrees. It was the first time that I was sad that the water was so warm! I needed to find a colder lake. I went to the owner of my Airbnb apartment and asked her for advice. She mentioned Achensee in Austria, which was not so far from the place where I was. For the next day, I planned my Achensee trip, checked everything in google maps, and decided to drive there. I was focused, I had driven all the way to Bayern; now I needed to find a place where I could do my qualifier.

22nd June 2019, Achensee, Austria, 13-14 degrees:
We drove to Achensee in Austria, which was 50 kilometers away from Tegernsee. Achensee was about 13-14 degrees. First, I thought, "Oh my God! It is colder than I expected, how can I handle this cold and swim for two hours?" 14.9 degrees would be enough for me, and now it was 13 degrees. Emre motivated me, and we prepared hot carbohydrate drinks. Eating is really important for cold water swims of more than an hour. You need proper hot food to stay warm. Every 30 minutes, we stopped briefly and drunk the hot drink, which gave us the power and inner fire to continue. It helped a lot mentally as well. I always focused on the next feed to motivate myself. If you think about the overall goal, the goal becomes bigger than you. But if you split your goal into smaller pieces, then it becomes easier to

handle, not only physically but mentally.

In the end, we swam 120 minutes in this beautiful cold lake between the Alps. I am so happy to have had this amazing experience. I couldn't believe that I had achieved it. Now, I was ready for the English Channel!

You have heard me say I was happy after each challenge, but that's exactly what I want to highlight in this book while you read my stories of determination.

The more you challenge yourself, the more you explore what you are capable of and feel strong, satisfied, and happy with yourself. Don't wait for the right moment. Start exploring yourself in different ways and follow your passion!

23rd June 2019, Day 2 Königsee, 10-11 degrees:
The owner of the Airbnb house had also recommended Königsee, a lake in the far southeast of the German state of Bavaria, near the Austrian border. This lake is famous as a nature reserve, where swimming is normally forbidden, and the water is freezingly cold. We swam without permission, but luckily, nobody told on us, and everything went well. We needed another challenge to explore our limits and extend our comfort zone further. So, we went to Königssee.

We swam in paradise for 62 minutes in 10-11 degrees of cold water. After our swim session, for the first time, I didn't have "the shakes." It was strange because the water was colder than Achensee, but I focused on controlling my body, and it helped. I could control my body with my mind.

This experience in the camp showed me that training is key, and with constant training and concentration, you can deal with the cold while getting stronger both mentally and physically. Going out of our comfort zone empowers us to deal with challenges better than we have ever done. I am happy to have gone into this beautiful place and have had this great experience.

The cold is in our mind. We can control our mind and body. Last year, I could not even imagine swimming in 11-degree water, and these past two days, I had swum for 1 and 2 hours in freezing water and could handle my mind and body. **Believe - Train - Achieve.**

HOW DID I DEAL WITH THE COLD WATER BESIDE MY TRAINING?

I am 1.66m tall and weigh just 54kg. Having some fat is useful in cold water acclimatization, but I didn't want to gain weight. Therefore, I decided to increase my brown fat level through continuous cold water immersions. Besides the targeted mental preparations, such as mediation, the Wim Hof breathing method, mindful nutrition, and regeneration, helped me get stronger and increase my resilience level.

Wim Hof Breathing Technique (https://www.wimhofmethod.com/)
Wim Hof, also known as The Iceman, is a Dutch extreme athlete noted for his ability to withstand extreme cold, which he attributes to his Wim Hof Method (WHM) breathing technique. His method enables you to manipulate your central nervous system, increase the PH level of your body, and boost your immune system as well as your energy level.

Wim Hof has a message for each of us:
"You can literally do the impossible. You can overcome disease, improve your mental health and physical performance, and even control your physiology so you can thrive in freezing temperatures." With the Wim Hof Method, this trailblazer of human potential shares a method that anyone can use—not just extreme athletes or spiritual masters—to supercharge your capacity for strength, health, and happiness.

His method is based on three powerful pillars, as summarized in his book *Becoming an Iceman*:

1. **Cold Therapy:** The cold is your warm friend and one of the three pillars of the Wim Hof Method. Proper exposure to the cold starts a cascade of health benefits, including the buildup of brown adipose tissue and resultant fat loss, reduced inflammation that facilitates a fortified immune system, balanced hormone levels, improved sleep quality, and the production of endorphins— the feel-good chemicals in the brain that naturally elevate your mood.

2. **Breathing:** The second pillar of the Wim Hof Method is breathing. We're always breathing, yet we're mostly unaware of its tremendous potential. Heightened oxygen levels hold a treasure trove of benefits, and the specialized breathing technique of the Wim Hof Method unearths them all: more energy and reduced stress levels, and an augmented immune response that swiftly deals with pathogens.

3. **Commitment:** The third pillar of the Wim Hof Method is the foundation for the other two: both cold exposure and conscious breathing require patience and dedication to be fully mastered. Armed with focus and determination, you are ready to explore and eventually master your own body and mind.

Wim Hof's method is so easy and effective to do, and his achievements are so inspiring. His story shows us how we can go out of our comfort zone, break our limits, and get stronger both mentally and psychically. There may be times when you don't feel happy, when you have the feeling that you are losing control of your life, when you feel depressed or need some new inspiration in your life. Wim Hof had hard times as well. He felt that he didn't understand the world anymore. He lost all control of his life when his wife decided to take her life suddenly. Wim Hof is proving to us that we can handle pain, and we can go out of our comfort zone and control our mind and body.

Here is the concrete description of the breathing exercise, which is described in his book *Never Sick Again* – let's try it!

1. **Controlled hyperventilation** -The first phase involves 30 cycles of breathing. Each cycle goes as follows: Take a powerful breath in, fully filling the lungs. Breathe out by passively releasing the breath, but not actively exhaling. Repeat this cycle at a steady rapid pace thirty times. Hof says that this form of hyperventilation may lead to tingling sensations or light-headedness.

2. **Exhalation** - After completion of the 30 cycles of controlled hyperventilation, take another deep breath in, and let it out completely. Hold the breath for as long as possible.

3. **Breath retention** - When a strong urge to breathe occurs, take a full deep breath in. Hold the breath for around 15 - 20 seconds and let it go. The body may experience a head-rush sensation, which is completely normal.

These three phases may be repeated for three consecutive rounds. For further information, you can check the YouTube videos "Guided Wim Hof Breathing." and his website: https://www.wimhofmethod.com/.

Please be aware of the safety regulations:

- Always do the breathing exercise in a safe environment and don't force your body.
- Don't do this exercise in a situation where it might be dangerous to faint. So don't do it in the water, in a bath or when driving a vehicle.

THE POWER OF VISUALIZATION – EVERYTHING STARTS IN YOUR MIND!

Besides training and breathing exercises, I strongly believe in "visualization," which works hand in hand with the Law of Attraction. The idea is to visualize an image in your head; by consistent visualization of this image, it will be attracted to you (How to Use the Power of Visualization - Mindvalley Blog. https://blog.mindvalley.com/the-power-of-visualization/).

You may have heard people say, I can't imagine riding 100 miles on my bike, performing on stage, painting a mural, etc. etc… They are never, ever, going to achieve these things because they are not capable of imagining themselves achieving them.

Everything that was ever created or achieved first started as an idea in someone's mind. Usually in response to some need or some desire, an idea took hold, and the person began focusing their mental energy on it. The idea built on itself as the mental energy became infused with emotions. This created a massive desire, and the person's mind went into overdrive, looking for ways to marry the vision with physical reality.

During my preparation for the Turkish and German championships, I always visualized the race and my performance beforehand. I was always nervous, and to deal with this state, I visualized the race many times in my mind. This helped me to prepare myself mentally. I used this technique for my cold water immersions as well. The visualization exercise is easy to start. You are sitting or lying in a comfortable position with your eyes closed. You visualize the exact location where you need to perform something. It can be a sports race, a presentation in front of senior people, a life performance, or just a new thing that you will try for the first time. Imagine what you wear, how you look like, the people around you, your feelings, your fears, in short, everything relating to the situation. And visualize how strong you are, how you deal with this specific challenge, and being successful at the end. Connect this visual element with positive affirmations. That was exactly what I tried to do beforehand. I thought about the cold water and how I would feel when in the water. I visualized that my mind was stronger than my body and that I would accept the cold and go in as a strong woman and start to swim. I imagined I would breathe in and breathe out to control my swim. I imagined that the sun heated and protected me. This kind of mental preparation helped me a lot to stay focused for the preparation of new challenges.

Start to visualize your dream, feel how you achieve your goal, and focus on that. Everything starts in your mind and becomes real in your life!

NUTRITION

What you eat and drink, and when, plays a big role in cold water immersion. For example, when you drink alcohol, you feel the cold water more than normal. Your body is weaker and less immune to cold. To gain brown fat and get more resistance to the cold, it is important to eat foods with a high amount of healthy fat like salmon, avocado, and nuts.

HERE IS A LIST OF MY TOP HEALTHY-FAT FOODS

Fish: Naturally fatty fish like salmon, mackerel, herring, lake trout, sardines, and albacore tuna are good sources of omega-3 fatty acids. These are "good" fats that help keep your heart healthy. They may also help keep your brain sharp, especially as you get older (Healthy Fat Foods for Your Diet - WebMD. https://www.webmd.com/diet/ss/slideshow-healthy-fat-foods).

Avocado: When you eat avocado with other foods, it helps your body absorb their nutrients better. Half a medium avocado is one serving and about 160 calories.

Nuts: From hazelnuts to pecans, all nuts are good for your heart. Walnuts, especially, deliver heart-healthy fats.

Eggs: Eggs are a great source of inexpensive protein. A large, hard-boiled egg has about 4.7 grams of fat, mostly healthy fats. Some eggs are also enriched with extra omega-3. It will say so on the box.

During a longer cold swim, eating is essential to keep you warm and energetic. Most people prefer their first feed 1.5-2 hours into their swim and then have a feed every 45 minutes to an hour. If you think you will be eating only a couple of times (which would be the case in a 10K event), then anything would probably work - energy gel, carb powder drink, etc... But for really long distances, you need to try out the food in a long practice swim beforehand to see if your body will accept it. And therefore, you should experiment with different types of food to see which one works best for you.

REGENERATION, ESPECIALLY SLEEPING

Sleep and nutrition are responsible for most of the recovery. There are very few other methods that actually work. Sleep plays an important role in keeping your mind strong so that you can deal with cold water. Every time, when I was tired and had less sleep, I felt the cold much more, and it was harder to deal with it. Don't forget that regeneration is as important as hard training. Balance is key. Garima Sharma explains that people who get less than 6 to 7 hours of sleep each night are at a greater risk of developing diseases. A good night's sleep makes you feel energized and alert the next day. Being engaged and active not only feels great but also increases your daily energy and helps you face cold water in a more relaxed manner.

Vaseline: For long open water swims, I cannot overemphasize the importance of Vaseline, at least in areas like armpits where you could get abrasion. And for colder water, I suggest mixing Vaseline and lanolin, what English Channel swimmers call "channel grease." Needless to say, you should try these at least a few times before your big swim day.

In summary, your mind should be ready, and in addition to the training, your body should be regenerated, with enough sleep and enough food in your body to go out of your comfort zone and face the challenge. Start to reflect on your regeneration activities. Are they enough? Do you have a balance? Start to take enough time for your recovery!

The cold water challenged me, but it also gave me a new dimension in my life. What exactly is happening when you are in cold water? What are the benefits of this? Here, you find the summary of the main benefits and effects in your life, as extracted from the Wim Hof book *Never Sick Again*:

BENEFITS OF COLD WATER

After my cold swim training, I continued to read Wim Hof's book *Never Sick Again*.

What are the benefits of cold immersion?

Reduced stress levels. Delray Beach Cryo of South Florida, the leading technology in Cryotherapy treatments, indicates that regularly taking cold showers imposes a small amount of stress on your body, which leads to a process called hardening. This means that your nervous system gradually gets used to handling moderate levels of stress. The hardening process helps you to keep a cool head the next time you find yourself in a stressful situation.

After my cold water swims, I have always felt that my stress level decreased. I became a calmer person, especially in stressful situations at work. While everybody around me became stressed because of some deadline or pitch, I had a general calmness and feeling that I could handle every challenge out of my comfort zone.

Higher level of alertness. Cold showers or swims wake your body up, inducing a higher state of alertness. The cold also stimulates you to take deeper breaths, decreasing the level of carbon dioxide throughout your body, helping you concentrate. Cold showers keep you ready and focused all day.

After cold immersions, I felt that I had started to become more efficient, focus much more, and had a higher level of concentration at work. I had a high energy level and felt less exhausted from working hard, both physically and mentally. I also had the feeling that I was more alert, could recognize hidden messages or energies, and demonstrated more sensibility toward people.

More robust immune response. Scientific studies have found that taking a cold shower increases the number of white blood cells in your body. These blood cells protect your body against diseases. Researchers believe that this process is related to an increased metabolic rate, which stimulates the immune response.

Normally, when you swim in winter in a lake, you would expect to get ill. For me, the opposite was the case. After those breathing exercises and cold immersions, I didn't become sick. On the contrary, my mind and body were stronger than before.

Increased willpower. It takes a strong mind to endure the cold for extended periods. By incorporating cold showers into your daily routine, you are strengthening your willpower, which benefits many aspects of your daily life.

The willpower and determination gave me the motivation to face other challenges in my life and deal with them in a more relaxed and confident way. I trusted myself more and had a more optimistic view of feeling pain. I had more hope and felt more enjoyment, even when I was facing internal and external hurdles.

Weight loss. Research has shown that cold showers (and exposure to cold in general), in addition to increasing metabolic rate directly, stimulate the generation of brown fat. Cold showers, then, are an effective tool for people who are looking to lose a few kilos.

After cold immersions, I felt my body more refreshed and firmed. Even my friends said that they saw a difference in my body. I had more muscle, a more toned body, and a stronger posture. Of course, body fat helps, as I explained above, and I tried to eat more to gain some weight, but cold water swims were burning more calories than normal exercise, and, in the end, I had the same weight, but just with a stronger body and mindset.

SUMMARY

1. **Tunnel vision can be dangerous.** Tunnel vision means that the edges of your vision are lost, and only central focus remains as if you are looking through a tunnel. It is a lack of perspective caused by an intense focus on one object, leading to the neglect of surroundings and responsibilities, or being closed off to other viewpoints.

2. **Pain is growth.** After pain, there come magical moments of growth, which are the special moments we need to enjoy. Without pain, no gain.

3. **Don't forget the power of visualization** - Everything starts in your mind! Believe in what you do, plan it in your mind, visualize and realize it.

4. **We can control our mind and body**. The cold and other challenges are in our minds. Use different techniques to strengthen your mind and body, and you will be surprised at what you are capable of.

5. **The more you have extraordinary goals in your life and do unique things, the more you are alone in your journey.** Don't be afraid to be alone and follow your passion. You have all the power, and you will always find people around you who share the same passion and similar journeys.

6. **Cold water immersions can change your life**. It can transform your body and brain. You feel refreshed, your brain can reboot, and your body will be more firmed.

7. **The benefits of cold immersion:**
   - ▶ Reduced stress levels
   - ▶ Higher level of alertness
   - ▶ More robust immune response.
   - ▶ Increased willpower
   - ▶ Weight loss.

8. **There are different definitions of cold water.** Most organizations define cold water as under 17 degrees Celsius. But most people feel cold under 21 degrees. The temperature of a swimming pool is, on average, 27 degrees.

9. **Sleep and nutrition are responsible for most of the recovery.** There are very few other methods that actually work. Sleep plays an important role in keeping your mind strong so that you can deal with cold water.

10. **What you eat and drink, and when, plays a big role in cold water immersion, and you can feel the direct effects in your body.**

10

Assignment in London - Change experience and road to the English Channel - Relay

In two months, we would swim in the English Channel. After all the preparation, our dream would finally come true.

My employer, EY, had sent me to London for three months to support the global enablement for a new Change Experience solution.

WHAT EXACTLY IS THE "CHANGE EXPERIENCE" SOLUTION ABOUT?

We are in a disruptive world; everything is changing. Transformation is no longer an option; it's a necessity in every part of our life. The Change Experience solution is a personalized and immersive approach to manage change in organizations. Informed by client experience and research from Harvard Business School, the Change Experience approach addresses four common factors that have the greatest influence on successful outcomes to transform the way the workforce experiences change and to empower them to achieve the extraordinary. A steady focus on the people's "experience" of change creates a powerful impact at every stage of the change journey, which drives better transformation outcomes. By combining a people-first stance with digital components, my colleagues and I analyze and provide insights that can help organizations adapt to – and even benefit from – the constant challenges of continuous change.

I was happy to have this opportunity to be in London, and as I worked on this exciting new project, I used the opportunity to swim at Dover over the weekends, where the English Channel swim starts. The timing couldn't have been better, as I could integrate my business and swimming goals. I had been to London several times before, but this time was truly unique. My company had arranged a nice apartment next to the Thames for me, and I had a great team with multinational colleagues.

But I was also faced with a major problem: There was no proper swimming pool near my home or office. The lidos closed around 7 p.m. I was usually working until later than that, and therefore, it had become a real problem to train. The Olympic swimming pool in the London Aquatics Centre, which is in Queen Elizabeth Olympic Park in Stratford, was open until 9 pm. The center, one of the main venues of the 2012 Summer Olympics and the 2012 Summer Paralympics, was used for the swimming, diving, and synchronized swimming events. After significant modification, it opened to the public in March 2014.

This was a great option, but it was 40 minutes away from my office in London Bridge. I decided to keep doing my mental preparation with the breathing exercises and run at least four times a week next to the Thames. The view was stunning. I trained 1-2 times a week in the pool, and the rest was just running and mental training.

But I felt ready for the English Channel. I had trained in Germany in the lakes and in Austria and Turkey throughout the winter and early spring. I used my time efficiently and did whatever I could alongside my hard consulting work.

I tried to stay fit through some pool training and running sessions. London was an out of comfort zone experience for me as well. The city was overwhelming and exciting after Frankfurt. The energy of the city and the people were amazing. The traffic was crazy. The business was also challenging: The team was new, the colleagues were new, from all over the world. It took me some time to adjust to this new environment and fast-working pace. The working hours were also different than in Germany. We had calls at 6 am and also at 11 pm. It wasn't easy to manage all the different expectations of various team members from all over the world. The environment was demanding, and the atmosphere in the business was sometimes tense because of miscommunication between different working styles. One night, I fell asleep on a call. I felt exhausted, and it was too much to handle swimming, business, and my private life challenges all at once.

Besides the demanding project time, I had met, in a short time, many different people and colleagues and had different after-work plans every day, including swimming and sports, but also hanging around in pubs and drinking beer with colleagues and friends. I was looking forward to doing the relay swim in the English Channel. Many people were asking me about the relay swim at this time.

WHAT EXACTLY DOES "RELAY CHANNEL SWIM" MEAN?

First of all, a "relay Channel swim," as the team effort is called, is really not that different from a solo. The distance is the same (a bit more than 32 kilometers), the rules are the same (no wetsuit, no touching the boat, etc.). The only difference is that the swimmers in the team take turns swimming: The team has to declare the order the swimmers will enter the water, and then, following that order, each swimmer has to spend one hour in the water. Once all the swimmers in the team have swum once, it is back to the first swimmer again, and this goes on until the crossing is complete.

Each team may consist of a minimum of two and a maximum of six swimmers. In a team of six decent swimmers, who can swim around 3 kilometers in an hour, each swimmer may expect to enter the water only twice. Our team, "Out of our comfort zone," was initially made up of four swimmers: Me, an Iranian Prof. Raha Akhavan from Sabanci University, Emre Deliveli, and Darren Watson. We expected to cover 12-13 kilometers each round, and this would mean that we would probably finish in the third round, and the last swimmer may not have the chance to enter the water for the third time.

Sounds like a walk in the park, or rather a swim in the pond? Well, not really... While a one-hour swim is no big deal by itself, it is the cold that bites. In the summer, water temperatures in the Channel range between 15 to 18 degrees, well below what many pool and open water swimmers are used to. And so, if you go to the Channel without acclimatizing yourself to cold water swimming, you may not be able to stay in the water for a full hour even if you have done marathon swims in the past. Moreover, while the human body adapts quite quickly to cold water swimming, as I was figuring out through my training, many relay Channel swimmers will tell you that waiting for your turn after your swim is actually more difficult than the swim itself: You feel extremely cold, and the boat offers little protection from the elements... if any. Throw in a rocking boat, and you'll enter the water for the second time shivering and seasick. And here is the most important catch: One of your teammates cannot swim on your behalf when your turn comes. If you don't/can't enter the water, your relay Channel swim is considered unsuccessful. Your team is expected to stick to the order they declared before their swim until the end.

As you can see, while it does not require the extreme cold water tolerance and physical and mental endurance of a solo Channel swim, a relay swim is no joke, either. Come ill-prepared, physically or mentally, and you could sink the whole team effort, and needless to say, on the ride back to Dover, you won't be the most popular person on the boat. That's why a relay performance puts pressure on all team members. If one fails, the whole team fails. Therefore, a relay swim is an intense teamwork experience, and you must consider the team dynamics even during the preparation.

We were all set for the English Channel. We had booked the hotel, I had arranged my holiday days with my company, we had our confirmation from the Channel Swimming Association, we had, of course, arranged the boat, and most importantly, we as a team were ready to start together. We were ready for the challenge, which would take place in 5 weeks.

TWO WEEKS LATER.

My team members and our coach had gone to Northern Ireland. Kamil Resa Alsaran, our coach and a successful open water swimmer himself, had already swum the English Channel twice, and he now wanted to swim the North Channel, from Northern Ireland to Scotland - thought by many to be one of the world's most challenging ultramarathon swims. The water temperature in the North Channel is around 12-13 degrees, and there are big toxic jellyfish. My team was there to support him and also to do a cold swim camp to prepare for the English Channel. They were also speaking of a relay North Channel swim, but I never took it seriously. I was new in London, I had a hectic job, and I was preparing myself for the English Channel, not for the tougher North Channel.

One day, my team wrote me via WhatsApp that they were planning to do a relay North Channel swim and that they wanted me to join them. I had never taken this plan seriously, and this time was no different. Me swimming in 12 degrees cold water without proper training? No way! If nothing else, they were there for at least one week, their body was getting used to cold water, and I was working in London, drinking beer, and only running instead of hard swim sessions. I told them that I could not join their relay swim, as it wouldn't make sense at this stage and that I was looking forward to our English Channel relay swim. For me, it would be a big challenge, not just physically but also professionally and financially: I would have to leave my job for a few days and incur additional costs. I didn't have any sponsors and had to pay for everything with my consulting salary. Even the channel relay swims costs around 3.000-4000 Euros without calculating the preparation costs. I, therefore, declined and hoped that they could understand my situation.

But my teammates could not do it without me: As a 3-person team, they would need to swim at least four times, based on a 12-hour swim. If I joined the team, then they would only need to swim just three times. A few hours later, our coach Kamil texted me and said that the team was waiting for me, and it was time now to prove my teamwork and myself in the cold water. I was so irritated. I felt alone and also felt the pressure from different angles. I spoke about my situation with my colleagues at work. Interestingly, they pushed me and encouraged me to fly to Ireland and face this challenge. They said that they could handle the work for two days, that and it would be OK if I took 1-2 days off. I thought that, maybe, this was a sign, and now I needed to act. I checked last-minute flights, spoke with my senior manager, tried to organize myself, and calmed down my parents, who were not happy about my risky plans. I knew that no matter how old I was, they would always be worried about me, and I needed to convince them about my plans.

SUMMARY

1. **We are in a disruptive world, everything is changing. Transformation is no longer an option; it's a necessity in every part of our life.** A steady focus on the employee's people's "experience" of change creates a powerful impact at every stage of the change journey, which drives better transformation outcomes.

2. **A "relay Channel swim,"** is really not that different from a solo. The distance is the same (a bit more than 32 kilometers), the rules are the same (no wetsuit, no touching the boat, etc.). The only difference is that the swimmers in the team take turns swimming: The team has to declare the order the swimmers will enter the water, and then, following that order, each swimmer has to spend one hour in the water. Once all the swimmers in the team have swum once, it is back to the first swimmer again-and this goes on until the crossing is complete.

3. **A relay swim is a team effort**. You need to plan with the team, motivate and trust each other. The more you train together and trust each other, the better you can face the challenge.

11

The freezing experience in the North Channel - Sometimes you are not following the flow; you are exactly the flow

A NEW (AND TOUGHER) CHALLENGE: THE NORTH CHANNEL SWIM

Sometimes you do not just follow the flow, you are part of the flow

It was less than one month until my English Channel relay swim with my team, "Out of Our Comfort Zone," and I suddenly have found myself in an even bigger challenge: A North Channel 5-person relay swim in the team, "Cilgin *Turkler*" (Mad Turks). Three members of my English Channel relay team, Emre Deliveli, Yasemin Akhavan, the first Turkish woman who swam Gibraltar, and Prof. Raha Akhavan, were already in the North Channel to support our English Channel coach Kamil Resa Alsaran's solo attempt, and they were part of the relay. Kamil, a two-time English Channel and Triple Crown (English Channel,

Catalina, Manhattan) swimmer, would probably be in our team as well.

The North Channel crossing is more or less the same distance as the English Channel. However, it is considered a much more difficult route for two reasons: First, the water temperature is several degrees lower; for example, whereas Dover is around 17 degrees at the end of July, my relay teammates had told me that the water temperature around Donaghadee Beach had been around 12-14 degrees for the past few days. Also, the lion's mane jellyfish in the North Channel have quite a bit more bite, or rather sting, than the ones in the English Channel. For these reasons, the North Channel was considered not swimmable, and it wasn't until 1947 when the first successful crossing was made; the next one did not happen until 1970. There are only around 80 successful solo swims to date compared to around 2,400 for the English Channel. The North Channel is considered by many as the toughest one of the **Ocean's Seven**. The cold water, the big jellyfish, the currents, and the unpredictable sea conditions make this route hard.

The logistics of the actual swim are actually very similar to the English Channel. You start outside the town of Donaghadee in Northern Ireland, and swim across, usually ending up near the Scottish town of Portpatrick. The rules for both the solo and relay crossings are quite similar as well - for example, just like in the English Channel, we would all be swimming for one hour in a predetermined order.

I flew to Belfast on July 26 to join my teammates. For me, doing this challenging swim was another step in my journey of cold water swims and being out of my comfort zone. Surprisingly, I was in the North Channel prior to my English Channel swim!

Sometimes, all energies bring you to that place where you are, and you not only follow the flow, you are part of the flow and unstoppable.

When I arrived at Donaghadee, it was late at night. The weather forecast did not look too good. The team told me that we might not be able to swim. I was so disappointed and thought that I had come for nothing. I had paid so much money for the last-minute plane ticket and had tried hard to arrange my work responsibilities, and now they were saying that we may not swim. I also had confused feelings. On the one hand, I wanted to face this challenge with my team, and on the other, I was really scared. I felt confused and had difficulties in regulating my feelings. The next morning, we woke up and went directly to the sea. When I measured the water temperature, it was 12 degrees. The water was freezing. When I tried to go in, my foot started tingling, I felt stitches on my skin, my heart rate increased, and I couldn't breathe properly because of the cold shock. It was tough. I swam with my team members and followed them. After 20 minutes, I became slower and slower. I was afraid of the toxic jellyfish. Ireland has five indigenous jellyfish species: Barrel, Blue, Common (Moon), Compass, and Lion's Mane! The majority of jellyfish have preferred habitats: The Lion's Mane jellyfish are the most common in the North Channel. They prefer the cooler waters of the Irish Sea and especially the waters off Dublin. I concentrated on checking for them to protect myself. My body started to shake because of the cold. I felt so bad. Mentally, I swam in this alert mood. I was afraid of the jellyfish, and at the same time, my body was giving me signals to get out. I fought with my mind and tried to stay positive, encouraging myself to swim for at least one hour. In case we were able to do the relay, I needed to be ready. I tried to use positive self-affirmations, tried to focus on solutions, followed my team members, and tried to stop my negative thoughts:

"It's cold. How will I swim for the next 30 minutes? I want to get out. What am I doing here? Am I crazy? Are we crazy? This is really overwhelming. What if a jellyfish touches me, and I get poisoned and cannot swim in the relay? What would I say to my mom and dad? What would I say to my boss? It's f.....g cold. How will I do the relay? I can't swim, I am getting slower and slower, shit."

With all those thoughts in my mind, and my deeper voice saying, "Let's do it. Continue. Don't give up. Come on. You can do it. You need to continue and get ready for your team," I completed one hour. After that, we immediately went home, and I had 40 minutes of shakes and drank a hot ginger lemon tea to return to normal. I felt demoralized. I didn't expect that the water would be so cold, and my body would react like this. When I slowed down so much after 20 minutes, and my fingers completely froze, how could I swim the relay? We had breakfast, and afterward, I went to my room and didn't speak to anybody for a few hours. I tried to sleep but couldn't. In the afternoon, we wanted to swim again for one hour. My brain and my body felt exhausted, and I felt insecure. After a few hours, we went out and walked to the beach for the next training session. This time, I felt much better in the water. At least, I could hold my pace. I still had the shakes after 45 minutes, but I could stay mentally stronger in the water. My negative thoughts were fewer, and my positive affirmations worked more. I felt empowered again. The second round of the day was, for sure, better than the first shocking round.

The day after, we had our a one-hour training again in the morning. In the afternoon, we met our captain, Richard Lafferty, of the Aquaholics boat. He said that we could swim the next day, as the weather looked better than before. That meant we would start our swim early Monday morning at around 4 am and end at night. My flight was the following day at 6 am because of an early project meeting in London. I was afraid I might not catch my flight. So, I felt pressured and prayed that everything would work fine.

I felt really nervous but was also happy that at least we could swim and not go back empty-handed.

We bought food for the boat, prepared everything, and had an early dinner. The house was silent. Everybody was nervous. Our coach, Kamil, would swim his solo the same day, which meant we had a 4-person relay team instead of 5. Good that I came;

otherwise, the team would have had just three members, making the swim very challenging for them.

The night was short. I couldn't sleep properly as I felt fear, concerns, and nervousness. I prayed often and tried to calm down. I did Wim Hof breathing and visualization exercises.

The alarm rang at 3 am. It was time to go. My bag was prepared. We had a quick breakfast—porridge with honey, nuts, banana, and hot ginger tea. Ruth Mccomiskey, a nurse from Bangor and part of our support team, who has a great, positive personality, picked us up and took us to the marina. The captain, Richard, Carmen Marquezaguilar from the support team, and our official observer were already there. We got to know each other and planned the next steps. Carmen was from Spain and was a heartful, sympathetic person. Ruth told me that she had a summer house in Datça, in my paradise. The crew was perfect. They motivated us from the beginning, made us smile, and reduced our stress. The swim started with Emre at around 6 am. Raha had the second round, and I had the third round. When I jumped into the water, I couldn't breathe. That's the first reaction when your body is in shock going into freezing water. I got a hot carb powder drink after 20 minutes, and the support team wrote motivational words on a whiteboard while I was swimming. In this kind of cold water, with dangerous jellyfish, you need real motivation and support.

DIVIDE YOUR GOAL INTO PIECES AND KEEP YOUR MIND MOTIVATED

You need to keep warm mentally, focus on good thoughts. The whiteboard helped me a lot to stay strong. Ruth and Carmen sang, danced; they did everything to keep our mood positive.

I can't forget one message on the board. Carmen painted a speed boat with the name "Deniz Line." Ruth and Carmen tried to motivate me with this drawing, and it really worked. The second message came from my mom: My mermaid, I am with you, sending you my love." All those messages kept my mind focused; the feeds helped a lot to divide the one hour into smaller pieces and continue the swim.

In our normal and corporate lives, it is also important to always split the big goal into smaller pieces. Then, you have the feeling you can handle it better step by step rather than thinking about the overall challenge.

I'd never had a swim like this in my life. We were alert all the time because of the jellyfish. Normally, if you swim long distance, you can swim in a flow and just continue without thinking or checking left or right. You are just following the boat, and that's it. But for this swim, we were checking for jellyfish all the time. The sun wasn't shining in the early morning. In the second and third rounds, the sun came, and with it, the jellyfish came closer to the surface. I had a big dilemma. When the sun was missing, it was really cold. The sun was warming my skin during the swim. But when the sun appeared, then the jellyfish risk increased as well. I was confused about what to wish for: The sun with the jellyfish or no sun with a colder challenge. In the second round of swimming, there were many lion's mane jellies. I thought I was in a minefield.

After the first one-hour swim, when I got out, I couldn't even change my swimsuit. My body shook like crazy, and my teammates, Yasemin and Raha, helped me put on warm clothes and drink hot ginger lemon tea. Without my teammates, I couldn't have survived. In this kind of extreme situation, you need all the support and motivation from your team. This immersive experience demonstrated great teamwork. The first hour after the swim is the worst because not only do you try to bring your body back to normal, you also need to get ready for the second round. At the same time, you are supporting your teammates in the water. It is a long process, and in this kind of long distance, you need to have high levels of both mental and physical endurance.

After the third round, I felt so exhausted and cold. I hoped that I would not have to get into the water again. We finally saw the Scottish coast, and I was grateful that there would be no need to jump into the water again for the fourth round. Our team demonstrated a good performance; we were fast and accomplished the distance within 12 hours. Emre went into the water for the fourth time, and we were allowed to swim to the coast together.

"WHERE DID YOU COME FROM? WE SWAM FROM IRELAND TO SCOTLAND!"

We were lucky that we arrived at a nice beach near Portpatrick. The world was ours when we arrived at the coast and felt the sand. A woman who was staying at a holiday cottage right by the beach came out and asked us where we came from. We said that we had swum from Ireland to Scotland! She couldn't believe it. She was excited as well; she took our pictures and a few selfies and shared our short celebration moment. We also saw a beautiful waterfall on the beach, and it was a magical moment in our life. We had done it, and we were proud of ourselves. As a team, we strengthened our relationship with this kind of immersive experience, and we realized how strong we were together. We went back to the boat and celebrated our achievement. In parallel, Kamil Resa Alsaran broke the Guinness record, completing his solo and becoming the oldest man to have swum the North Channel.

We arrived home at around midnight. My flight was at 7 am, so I slept for just three hours before going to the airport. I had a meeting at 9.30 am and went directly from the airport to the office. It felt so strange. I felt like a fish out of water. I also felt like a solider had who won a war but continued with her normal life as if nothing had happened. For a few days, I took time to reflect on the immersive experience in order to balance my body and mind, to feel normal.

YOUR BRAIN IS YOUR LIMIT.

This experience showed me that, despite your fears, you should go for your goals. Your brain is your limit. Don't stop yourself, go for what you want to do, and you will see how magic will happen in your life! Start today to take action for your magical achievements and realizing your dreams!

"Impossible is nothing." There are no limits to what you can accomplish except the limits you place on your own thinking. Nothing can stop you!

SUMMARY

1. **Sometimes you do not just follow the flow, you are part of the flow.** Sometimes, all energies bring you to that place where you are, and you not only follow the flow - you are part of the flow and unstoppable.

2. **Your mind is your limit.** Despite your fears, you should go for your goals. Don't stop yourself, go for what you want to do, and you will see how magic will happen in your life! Start today to take action for your magical achievements and realizing your dreams!

3. **"Impossible is nothing."** There are no limits to what you can accomplish except the limits you place on your own thinking. Nothing can stop you!

12

Transformation from out of the comfort zone to the growth zone – The English Channel swim – Swimming for a good cause

After the out of comfort zone experience in the North Channel, I knew that it would be easier for all of us to handle the cold water in the English Channel. Compared to the North Channel, the water there is around 3-4 degrees warmer, and there are no toxic jellyfish. I felt less nervous and had the feeling that I had expanded my out of comfort zone into a growth zone, where I felt more secure, more experienced, and empowered to face the challenge. That's exactly what happens when you face new challenges in your private or corporate life as well. The more you go out of your comfort zone, the more you will expand your growth zone because the second time you have a similar challenge in your life, you will feel more comfortable and less nervous.

HARMONY ALWAYS PLAYS A BIG ROLE IN OUR LIVES

During this time, I kept in touch with my English Channel and North Channel team members on WhatsApp. There are so many WhatsApp groups, and sometimes you lose control of all the messages. It was exactly one day like this, where I was so busy and had many things to do, I realized that our team would now be 5-person instead of 4-person. I was shocked. That meant I would maybe swim just two times instead of three. I felt so angry and asked my teammates why they had taken this kind of decision without asking me properly.

We had some discussion, and after some back and forth, one team member, Darren, decided to quit the team. After that, Emre also decided to quit the team.

It was a crazy situation. We had turned from a 4-person team to a 5 -person team and then to a 3-person team in a matter of days. A 3-person team would mean I would need to swim four times in freezing water.

My stress level was high anyway. A new role in London, a new environment, new colleagues, and on top of all that, the swim challenge was on my mind. And now the team was changing a few weeks before the swim, and we were trying to figure out personal issues. What a week. In a relay swim, you need to trust all team members and must have full harmony to support each other properly. I felt so frustrated and tried to calm down. A few days later, Emre called me and said that he would continue as planned with us. Now, we were a 4-person team again, as planned, but with a different line-up. Darren was out, and Yasemin, with whom we swam the North Channel, was in.

We had been looking for a charity to support our English Channel swim for some time. After careful consideration, we decided to go with Cagdas Yasami Destekleme Dernegi (CYDD) - Association for Supporting Contemporary Life- and collect money for them. This NGO has projects for education in Turkey, mainly the education of girls. Through our swim, we would raise funds for their university scholarship, which is called "you can light a candle, too." This initiative gave us an overall purpose. The swim wasn't just for us, it was also for young Turks who could not afford to go to college.

DOVER- DAY 1, AUGUST 21, 2019

I arrived in Dover, and I met my teammates at our guesthouse - Churchill Guest House, a lovely place near the beach. One of my teammates, Emre Deliveli, would swim his solo before our relay swim, and our team "out of our comfort zone" would probably swim the next day. Between these two swims, we would then have only three hours of sleep. We would also be in the solo boat to support him and swim with him. For sure, the hardest part would be for Emre, who would swim nonstop for more than 12 hours and then do the relay with us. In the hotel, we met a group from Mexico, who would also cross the English Channel. The mother of two great boys, Fiona Gomez Counahan, was there to swim her solo swim. The famous Mexican swimmer, Nora Toledano, who has completed Oceans Seven, the swimming equivalent of the Seven Summits, was there to coach her. Esteban Riva Palacio and Jose Ignacio Nacho were also there to support their mom. I felt so emotional when I saw them and hoped that everything would work out fine for them and that they would see Fiona complete her Channel swim.

In the afternoon, we went to the beach and trained for one hour. The water was about 18 degrees. I had the chance to swim with Nora. She was a great pacemaker for me, and we swam 4 km in 65 minutes. After our swim, I interviewed her for my website.

Our relay team "out of our comfort zone," Emre Deliveli, Raha Akhavan, and Yasemin Ayse, Yasemin Bagana, and our coach Kamil Resa Alsaran were looking forward to crossing the channel on Friday! I would start the swim at about 3 am, and then we would have the following swim order: Raha, Yasemin, Emre. We would be 3-4 times in the water and swim for one hour each.

DAY 2 AUGUST 22, 2019

We trained again in the Dover Harbor beach, and the water felt colder for me. It was wavy and windy. We became a little bit nervous. We completed our shopping afterward and bought everything we needed for our swim. Many bottles of water, tea, chocolates, sandwiches, painkillers, energy drinks, honey, and lots of snacks. We were ready for our challenge. In the evening, the captain said that we needed to change our plans. There is almost always a surprise when you decide to swim the English Channel. You need to check nature, and that means the waves, the currents, the wind, and much more. That's why many people have a slot of 7 days, and they stay in Dover without knowing their day to swim. The new plan was that Emre would swim his solo on Friday, and we would swim our relay on Sunday. This was actually good news for us because we would have at least 20 hours of rest between the solo and relay swims.

DAY 3 - TODAY/TOMORROW: SOLO START AT ABOUT 2 AM, AUGUST 23, 2019

Saturday night - Sunday morning: relay starts at about 3-4 am.

After we returned to our guesthouse, we saw the Mexican family. Fiona had completed her solo swim! She had realized her dream. It was so inspiring to see her, and we all celebrated and shared this unique moment.

Day 3 Thursday: Our teammate Emre would start tonight! We would leave our guesthouse at 1:15 am. During the day, we swam again with Nora. Afterward, we went shopping again, slept a little bit, and after dinner, we tried to sleep again for 2 hours before going to the Dover Marina for the start. It was exciting, and we were, of course, a little bit nervous. We are a great team- and we're stronger together.

This shared journey is not about just swimming. It's more about mental endurance as well as cooperation, supporting each other, and being strong as a team.

DAY 4 DOVER - EMRE DELIVELI IS AN "ENGLISH CHANNEL SWIMMER!" AUGUST 24, 2019

It was a hard and amazing day! We left the house at 1:15 am and went to the Dover Marina. Emre Deliveli started his solo at about 3 am. We supported him as a team and went in the water with him for one hour each. In the beginning, we all got seasick except our coach Kamil. Emre swam for 15 hours, 41 minutes and arrived in France! In his last meters, one person was allowed to swim with him to France. Kamil wanted to swim, but then he looked into my eyes and saw how willing I was to swim the last meters and be on this journey with Emre. He then said that I needed to get into the water. I had started on this journey with him, decided to swim the English Channel with him, and I needed to be there in the water with him. It was a meaningful moment for me. I couldn't say no, and I jumped into the water. There were several rules to follow:

- No touching
- I needed to swim behind or next to the swimmer
- No swimming in front of the swimmer

It was hard to control and adapt my pace and slow down for him. When we were near the beach, Emre wanted to hug me, but I swam away, trying to keep my distance in order to protect him. Otherwise, he could be disqualified. When he arrived at the beach, I went to him and hugged him. I was so proud of him and happy to see how his journey had ended successfully. Swimming is an individual sport, but this journey with Emre and my teammates taught me to take care of others, being happy with the success of others, sharing the moments, supporting each other more than ever. What an inspiration. He had started swimming just two years ago and crossed the English Channel. An example of dedication, focus, and hard work.

DAY 6, AUGUST 26, 2019, WE ARE ENGLISH CHANNEL RELAY SWIMMERS!

We started at 4.30 am, and I had the chance to be the first swimmer and swim from the dark into the sunrise. I put Vaseline all over my body. It was completely dark, and the captain told me to swim to the beach, get out of the water, and wave to the boat. Then, the official start would be given. I was so nervous, and at the same time, excited. I wanted to jump in the water, but I couldn't see the beach. The captain turned on his light and showed me the direction of the coast. I started to swim in the darkness and arrived at the beach. I heard the horn of the boat and started the swim. It was so magical. I felt so free and so powerful. Nature gave me the power, and I felt so grateful that I was realizing my dream. The team was there, the coach was there, everything went perfectly. Everything became real. I saw the sun rising slowly and focused on it. I felt a part of nature.

After me, Raha Akhavan was in the water, then Yasemin Bagana, and then Emre Deliveli. Each of us was in the water four times. The water temperature was about 18-19 degrees. After the North Channel experience, we could say "nice and warm." We were really lucky with the weather. The sun was shining all the time, and we were in a really good mood. Emre, who had swum his solo two days before, was still a little bit tired, but despite his pain, he gave everything for his team. Kamil Resa Alsaran observed us all the time and supported us.

In the last round, we were allowed to swim as a group to the coast. There were big rocks, where we took one selfie, and then we swam back to the boat.

We crossed the Channel in 11 hours 41 minutes, all the way from Dover to Cape Gris-Nez, the closest point in France to England. It was an amazing experience. My team and I felt the extended comfort zone after the North Channel experience. We were proud of ourselves and celebrated our achievement with champagne. These moments matter. I will never forget how we hugged each other on the coast. At the same time, we were able to collect donations for one of the biggest NGOs in Turkey.

TRANSFORMING YOURSELF IS THE HARDEST THING IN THE WORLD

The preparation for this journey and my experiences inspired me in my corporate life as well. This journey is not just about swimming. It is more about mental endurance, following your passion, supporting each other, being stronger as a team and exploring your potential, while going through an individual change experience. In my corporate life, I transform companies by managing change projects, and with this experience, I felt my individual transformation and change process. I recognized that it was actually much harder to transform myself compared to transforming others. Each change experience starts and ends in our individual transformation process.

SUMMARY

1. **Harmony always plays a big role in our lives.** In every challenge, you need to trust all team members and must have full harmony to support each other properly.

2. **Swimming is an individual sport,** but this journey with my teammates taught me to take care of others, being happy with the success of others, sharing the moments, supporting each other more than ever.

3. **Transforming yourself is the hardest thing in the world.** I recognized that it was actually much harder to transform myself compared to transforming others. Each change experience starts and ends in our individual transformation process.

4. **The key to success in the relay swim is not just about swimming.** This shared journey is not about just swimming. It's more about mental endurance as well as cooperation, supporting each other, and being strong as a team.

13

World championship with a piece of glass in my bone – December 2019

After a morning swim at the local pool in Frankfurt at the end of September, I had a bike accident on the road to my home: I collided with another bike and fell hard. My foot started bleeding. I felt a deep pain in my bone and started crying. It was a shocking moment for me. I didn't expect this kind of accident. Luckily, nothing seemed to be broken. I went to an emergency room. They checked my foot with an X-ray and didn't see anything in my bone. I ended up with stitches on my right ankle. Everything seemed fine. I had regular checks every week, and a few weeks later, they removed the stitches. Six weeks after this, I visited my friend at Usedom Island and decided to go for a run. I ran from Usedom to Poland, but I felt severe pain in my foot afterward. I realized that something was still wrong with my foot. But right after the running session, I was in 8 degrees of cold water and forgot about the pain.

Day by day, I started feeling that there was something really wrong. I went to a doctor again, and this time, they checked my foot with a Magnetic Resonance Imaging (MRI) scan. They saw something in my bone, which looked like a nail, but nobody was sure. I thought, "Is this a joke?" The doctors were not sure; they could not identify the foreign object. They checked it again with another method. In the end, they said that whatever it was, it needed to be removed and that I needed surgery. At first, I was devastated by the news, as the operation would mean that I would miss the Oceanman World Championships in Mexico in December. I had qualified for the event in May in Alanya, Turkey, after becoming third overall in women (first in my age category, first among Turks) in the 10-kilometer open water race. I decided to postpone the operation and not give up: I talked to the doctors, and it seemed there was little risk in postponing the operation. There was a small chance of infection, but this was a risk I could accept. The desire to join the world championship was greater than my fear. I hoped that my foot would be fine until Mexico; I was still training despite chronic pains in my foot. Even then, I reminded myself to be strong, never to give up, and keep smiling. It's hard to motivate yourself in these kinds of situations. Living with the risk, with the pain. Some people may think: Why are you doing this, is it worth it?

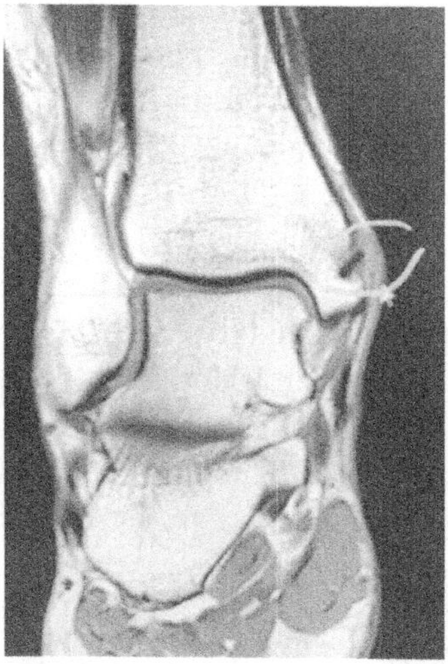

Success is a journey, not a destination. The journey is more important than the outcome. Go for it!

I thought, YES. I was still following my passion, hoped that all would work out well, and in the end, I would have a healthy foot again. I didn´t know how I would do in the race, but it didn't matter. What mattered was that I was on this journey with so many great people from all over the world.

Never give up and believe in yourself, keep smiling, and show the courage to go your way.

A few weeks later, I flew to Mexico. The Oceanman World Championship series took place in 16 countries in 2019 and is one of the largest open water swimming championships in the world. I met so many great people from all over the world. Almost all the swimmers stayed at the same hotel. My swimmer friends from Turkey were there, and Esteban from Mexico, whom I had met in Dover, was also there. I felt so happy. It was a feeling like meeting your extended family in one place and having fun, sharing great moments, and passion. It was an amazing organization and a great team spirit.

Before the race, we had so much fun with our swim group and visited some tourist attractions as well. We went to the Isla de Mujeres (women's island), Chichen Itza, the most famous of all the great Mayan cities, and also to Tulum, where we saw the beautiful ruins with views of the Caribbean. After Tulum, we spent some time in the nearby Paradise Beach.

THE GRAND FINALE – FULL OCEANMAN 10 KM

The day before the race, we had a ceremony where we represented our countries and had a race briefing session. Unfortunately, I was feeling very ill and weak. I had some stomach problems, flu, and chronic pains in my foot. All the symptoms came together. Despite the pain, I decided to swim, and I took painkillers. I knew that it wasn't the healthiest thing to do before a race, but I had no other option. I just wanted to attend this grand finale and believed that I would manage my body and my pain well enough to participate in the race and survive.

The 10-kilometer route was well-planned. We swam against the current during the first half of the race, and it was challenging to handle the hot water and weather. The water temperature was about 27 degrees, and the outside temperature about 29 degrees. I drank water only once. After 1.5 hours, I started to feel pain in my body. The effect of the painkillers was fading, and my foot was also hurting. But the swimming route was amazing. I saw beautiful fish and swam along with other swimmers. I tried to focus on the beauty, and not on what I was feeling in my body. Not being alone in the water and feeling nature motivated me and gave me the power to continue. The current was powerful and took all my energy. The return was much easier, but I was dehydrated and felt ill. I tried to focus, watching the nice houses on the beach, and I swam with two Mexicans next to me. I followed the red buoys, but it was hard to see the finish line. I fought against my pain continuously. One of the Mexicans started passing me, which was a sign that I was getting slower and slower. Thankfully, I had one energy gel with me and took it for the last minutes. After 3 hours and 11 minutes, I finished the race. When I got out, I couldn't walk; my right leg was so painful. Thankfully, Fermin Egido, the CEO of Oceanman, who is also a psychologist and sports enthusiast like me, gave me ice for my leg. Özkan Dizar, a Turkish pilot and ironman who had the 5th place in his age category, gave me water and a banana. I was really at the end of my limits, but happy to have had this experience, and finished the race as the 7th fastest woman in my age category. Despite the pain and dehydration, it was worth every second! I felt proud to be the 7th fastest woman from all over the world despite the circumstances.

Are you curious about what was in my bone? After the race and Christmas, I had the surgery. A piece of the lamp from the bicycle had gone into my bone. What a crazy accident!

Despite all the hurdles, follow your passion – share your passion and feel the experience!

SUMMARY

1. **Success is a journey, not a destination.** The journey is more important than the outcome. Go for it! Never give up and believe in yourself, keep smiling, and show the courage to go your way. Enjoy every moment on your way. Be aware that there will be some ups and downs. Accept those, and keep enjoying your journey.

2. **Despite all the hurdles, follow your passion** - share your passion and feel the experience! The goal is not always to be number one; sometimes, it's the achievement itself, to continue on your way and feel the experience. Don't always measure yourself by your results. Measure yourself by your mindset, by your coping strategies, and how you handle the situation. Your body, soul, and mind will tell you what to do and what feels right.

14

From fear zone to growth zone in South Africa - The way from Germany to South Africa, Johannesburg - One of the most dangerous cities in the world! February 2020

In addition to my swimming challenges, I have also been searching for out of comfort zone experiences in my consulting life. Different projects, different clients, and new challenges are always exciting. But to learn completely new cultures and to live in an environment completely new to you is the best out of comfort zone experience you can hope for. Therefore, I applied for an international assignment within my company in early 2019. I needed new perspectives, new inspiration sources for my life. I searched different offices, reached out to local partners, and had many interviews worldwide. My interview journey started in Sydney, continued in Singapore, and then New York. I waited several months for their replies, and during my change management project in London, I met Kate Skinstad, a Senior Manager from Johannesburg. She recommended for me to apply to South Africa and provided me with the main contacts. It was destiny. I never had South Africa in my mind. I was just focused on going to Australia, Asia, or the United States. After she gave me the contacts, I thought that this could be a spiritual sign, which I needed to follow. I also had nothing to lose and wanted to try this opportunity. I contacted the South African partner, and within two weeks, he got back to me, telling me that he liked my profile and that we could find a way to bring me to South Africa. As a sea lover and a passionate competitive open water swimmer, I wanted to go to Cape Town. In the end, the offer turned out to be for Johannesburg, where my firm's business is most active. Many friends told me it would be crazy to leave my good and safe life in Frankfurt, Germany, to go to South Africa, especially Johannesburg. In Germany, I was in my comfort area, but I wanted to leave this comfort zone by going to one of the most dangerous business cities in the world. Johannesburg was my fear zone. The zone that is insecure, for me, where I don't know how to handle specific situations, where I don't know trusted people and the patterns of the city. Where everything is new, where you need to follow new rules and need to show new behavioral patterns.

I came as an ex-pat to South Africa to manage big change projects for my company. Many people didn't understand why I chose to stay in Johannesburg, in one of the most dangerous cities in the world.

JOHANNESBURG, THE MOST DANGEROUS CITY ON EARTH?

South Africa's population is a unique mix of Africans, Europeans, and Asians, who speak one or more of the 11 official languages. Out of the total South African population of approximately 57 million, 44 million are black South Africans, 4.6 million are of mixed race, and 1.3 million are of Indian or Asian descent. The white population is 4.8 million (8% of the total population) and descends mainly from Dutch, German, French, and British colonial immigrants who came to settle in the country between the 17th and 19th centuries. South Africa has ranked as the third most dangerous country in the world, according to Numbeo's 2020 crime index, **with four cities among the ten most dangerous globally.** In a city with the world's fastest-rising rate of AIDS, this high crime rate has a terrifying extra dimension. And there's little the police can do. The chances of being murdered or raped in Johannesburg are significantly higher than almost anywhere else in the developed world. The chances of being robbed, mugged, held up, bag-snatched, or pick-pocketed are also much higher, with about 300 robberies a day. Johannesburg has a lot of tension between the citizens because of significant inequality.

When I decided to come to Johannesburg, my company provided me with special security training and many checklists with specific rules that I needed to follow.

One of my welcome emails covered a summary of some safety hints:

SAFETY TIPS FOR SOUTH AFRICA

Welcome to the rainbow nation of South Africa. These safety tips are provided for your safety and that of your loved ones. These tips are meant to help you, not scare you, so please read them carefully, but do not panic!

GENERAL SAFETY TIPS

- Do not attract unwarranted attention by openly displaying cash, expensive jewelry, cameras, and other valuables
- Carry your wallet, credit cards, passport, and other travel documents in your inside and front pockets
- Avoid carrying large sums of money, particularly foreign currency
- Avoid strange, dark, poorly illuminated, or isolated places
- Avoid traveling and exploring on your own
- Plan your travel routes beforehand

- Carry certified copies of your passport, ID, and travel documents
- Tag your luggage and belongings for easy identification and contract procedures

MOTOR VEHICLE SAFETY TIPS

Follow the applicable general tips above.

As in anywhere in the world, remember that your personal safety in a vehicle is strongly dependent on YOU. Make sure:

- All windows are fully closed
- Doors are locked
- Gearlock is secured when parked
- Alarm is switched on
- Valuables are locked away AT ALL TIMES, EVEN WHEN TRAVELING!
- Plan your route in advance
- Ensure you have sufficient fuel and that your vehicle is in a roadworthy condition
- Fasten your seatbelt, lock your doors, and keep your windows shut
- Avoid displaying valuables openly in the vehicle to avoid smash-and-grab crime. Lock your valuables in the boot (trunk).
- Be alert at traffic lights and stop streets. Leave enough space around the vehicle for a quick getaway.
- If you are softly bumped from behind, and the individuals involved look suspect, proceed to the nearest police station to report the incident - do not get out of the car.
- NEVER pick up strangers
- At night, park in well-illuminated areas. When returning to your vehicle, have your keys ready to unlock your car.

ON THE STREET

- Follow the applicable general tips above
- If possible, plan your route before
- Where possible, explore the streets in groups and stick to well-illuminated, busy streets
- Beware of your surroundings, be alert
- Walk on or close to the curb and face on-coming traffic. Avoid alley-ways and dense shrubs/bushes
- Use credit cards instead of cash where possible
- Avoid ostentatious displays of wealth
- If you require any information, approach a policeman, traffic officer, security officer, or shopkeeper.
- Avoid jogging or cycling alone and at night - plan your route beforehand. Vary your daily routine.
- Should you wish to use a taxi, your hotel or the local tourist information center will recommend a reliable service for you.

HOW TO REACT IN AN EMERGENCY

- Do not panic. Think laterally. Talk your way out of the situation.
- Do not resist unless you know that such resistance will lead to your escape.
- If your instincts are to physically resist do not hold back.
- If circumstances dictate that you must not resist, concentrate on noting the physical description and other notable features of your attacker.
- In a robbery or hi-jacking situation do as you are told. Do not argue or challenge your attacker and do not look directly into his eyes. Keep your hands still and visible. If you need to undo a seatbelt, ask first.
- Remember, you can replace your valuables and your vehicle, but not your life.

How would you feel after reading this welcome mail?

In the security training, the first question was: Why Johannesburg? Are you aware of what is waiting for you?

I became a little bit nervous and said: "Yes, I think so." After the call, I felt nervous but also had more respect than ever to where I was going. I thought: "When other people can go and live there, why can't I do it? If others can do it, I can as well." And I felt more excited than ever because I knew that this would be a completely different experience and exactly what I wanted: New experiences out of my comfort zone to gain new impulses, inspirations for my life. Even if it was in my fear zone, I knew that I would handle my fears and grow in this new environment.

FEBRUARY 2020 – MY FIRST WEEKS

When I arrived in Johannesburg, I was so afraid. The driver from the company picked me up, and I needed to pick up my house keys from the office. When we were there, I was afraid to walk by myself to the office. I asked the guy to come with me everywhere until I arrived at my home. I then locked all the doors and hid my laptop and my bag in the house in case somebody came and wanted to steal something. I felt I was being paranoid. I was also afraid to go by myself to the office. I called up a colleague and asked if she could pick me up so that we could go to the office together. I literally felt like a small kid who could not go outside alone. It felt so strange because, normally, I am a free bird and am not afraid of walking on the street on my own at night.

When I went shopping, I always hid my bag, and I was always on the alert. Driving was also a challenge. I was used to driving on the right. My first project was in the public transportation sector in Pretoria. I managed a transformation project and needed to go to the client site in Pretoria on my third day. The first time driving on the left at 60 km/hour, I felt so nervous. After a few days, I felt more relaxed than that first day.

Load shedding was also common. This means that the electricity in the city was cut off at certain times of the day. The traffic lights do not work during load shedding. Driving without knowing when it was going to happen was a challenge for me as well.

The work culture was more relationship-oriented, which felt a bit like Turkish culture. Therefore, I didn't have much difficulty adapting to that aspect.

FROM FEAR ZONE TO GROWTH ZONE

I decided to socialize quickly to get to know people with whom I could explore the beautiful country and do something. The clubhouse in my complex became very useful in socializing with my neighbors Darren, Dünyel Mcwade, Marcos Sousa, Mie Maya Mia, Kerry, Meltem, and Tonguc. In a short time, I was able to build a nice, colorful network.

I also got used to driving on the left side of the road and handling the traffic, even when the traffic lights were not working. I got a membership for one of the best gyms in the Sandton area and became a member of the Sandton Seal Swimming Club. I started to train and could organize my life within a couple of weeks. I felt much more comfortable after I had built a network, found places to exercise, and safe places where I could go to meet with friends and go shopping.

JUNE 2020 – AFTER THREE MONTHS

After three months, I even started to run on the street in the mornings. I expanded my comfort area and felt at home. I didn't have any fear anymore and felt in control.

Everything that I heard or checked in the media was partially right, but I was also surprised by this beautiful and comfortable life here and appreciated every second of my time in Johannesburg. I felt stronger than ever. If I had obeyed my fears, I wouldn't have come to this beautiful country and experienced what it offered me. The more I faced my fears and gave the city a chance, the more I felt powerful and comfortable. I saw that nothing is so bad compared to what we think, see in the media, or hear from others.

ALWAYS HAVE THE COURAGE TO EXPLORE, AND MAGIC CAN HAPPEN.

This city and all my experiences in South Africa gave me a completely different perspective regarding my private, social, and corporate lives. I explored different dimensions of other people and myself. Sometimes, we are looking for magic from outside, but the biggest magic is your own transformation. Knowing yourself a little bit more, exploring what you are capable of. This is the real magic, which leads to further enchanting moments with your family, friends, and colleagues in your life!

SUMMARY

1. **From Fear Zone to Growth Zone:** When you have the courage to face your fears and take risks, life will show you different dimensions, you will expand your perspectives, learn new things, and continue in the growth zone, which is not your discomfort zone anymore.

2. **Always have the courage to explore, and magic can happen.** Don't limit yourself in the comfort area. Explore new dimensions, cultures, and be open to new places. **South Africa**

3. **Sometimes, we are looking for magic from outside, but the biggest magic is your own transformation.** Knowing yourself a little bit more, exploring what you are capable of. This is the real magic, which leads to further enchanting moments with your family, friends, and colleagues in your life!

15

Breaking your limits and biggest fears by facing them- and just go for it from Robben Island to Cape Town

Don´t be afraid to go out of your comfort zone and face your fears. Desire, determination, and taking risks, despite the possibility of failing, make you stronger, and push your growth zone.

Living in Johannesburg was already out of my comfort zone, but I managed to find yet a higher level of out of comfort zone experience. The Robben Island swim.

I wanted to go further out of my comfort zone and expand my growth zone. I decided to try the Robben Island swim, one of the toughest open water routes in the world. It is famous for its freezing water and great white sharks. Robben Island is an island in Table Bay, around 7-8 kilometers west of the coast of Bloubergstrand, Cape Town, South Africa, and was the prison where Nelson Mandela was held for many years.

I have always been afraid of sharks, and almost everybody around me wanted to stop me from facing this challenge: " It is dangerous. Without cold training, it will be difficult. There are sharks, are you crazy?" and further limiting statements. All these limiting beliefs affect our lives, and I am using this swim experience as a metaphor. Don't listen to others' limiting thoughts. The more you face your fears, the more you feel free, powerful, and resilient.

Through my friend, Raymond de Villiers, who is a futurist helping clients to transform themselves, I found the best guy to help me face this challenge. Ryan Stamrood, who is a motivational speaker, has swum this route 109 times and is the world record holder for most Robben Island swims. I contacted him and asked him to swim with me. We met in Cape Town for a test swim in Big Bay. He was faster than me, for sure. Nevertheless, we decided to try it together and found a swim slot. I registered with the Big Bay Swimming Association and was able to get my hands on a shark banz, which would hopefully protect me from great whites. Sharkbanz is a rubber band that resembles a FitBit bracelet – uses a magnetic field to repel sharks by disrupting their electro-receptors, which they use to figure out that something is in the water.

A few weeks later, I went to Cape Town for the swim. Day one was freezing. The water temperature was 12 degrees. After half an hour, I got out and had the shakes for 40 minutes. I felt so demoralized. How could I swim in this water for 2.5 hours when I could not even manage to stay for more than 30 minutes?

I couldn't train enough in the cold water for this swim. You should not swim these kinds of long distances in such cold water temperatures without proper training. I prepared myself mentally. I was hoping that that the water would get warmer in the next 24 hours. Luckily, that turned out to be the case. Saturday morning, we checked the water temperature, and it was around 15 degrees. So, we decided to swim. The weather conditions weren't so great. There was no visibility, no sun. We couldn't even see the island. But after knowing that the water temperature was 15 degrees, I trusted myself, Ryan, the crew, and the process. I just focused on our goal and blocked all negative thoughts.

We went with the boat to Robben Island. We couldn't even see the island, and the captain turned on the GPS to ensure we were going in the right direction.

When we arrived at the island, I saw the kelp. I was
into the water. It was dark, cold, and scary. Ryan j
the water, and I jumped after him. We needed to get
near the shore to have an official start. I was so happy
follow Ryan. His presence decreased my anxiety before the challenge. When we swam past the kelp, I felt relieved and started to enjoy the swim. I trusted the shark shield and didn't think about the great whites at all. The swim took us 2 hours and 28 minutes, and I enjoyed every second. Every 30 minutes, I drank hot carb powder to feel the warmness in my body and get the energy to deal with the extremely cold water. During our swim, we saw some seals. I thought I saw a dolphin, my favorite animal. Ryan swam next to me all the time, but he was faster. To protect his body heat, he did some circles around the boat and me. Every time he was next to me, I felt motivated and got additional power to continue. It was cold, yes. It was challenging, yes. I can't describe the happiness I felt when I saw a stand-up paddler next to us. When the observer had said, a few minutes earlier, that we were nearly at the shore, I hadn't believed it and had thought they were saying this just to motivate me. But the stand-up paddler proved that we were indeed near the beach. That was the moment I believed that we were almost there. The misty weather didn't allow us to see the shore and Table Mountain. When I felt the sand under my feet, the world was mine. Kumar Uptal, my friend from Johannesburg, a successful sales manager originally from India who has worked all over the world, was there to support me and was waiting for me with a cup of hot chocolate. Carina Bruwer, the famous open water swimmer, acclaimed flute virtuoso, and founder of the internationally renowned instrumental group Sterling EQ, waited for us as well with a towel. I had met Carina in Turkey in the Aquamasters Swimming Cup. It was great to see her again in this kind of special moment and feel her support and excitement. Many other people also watched us and congratulated us. Wow, I had done it! I was proud to be the first Turkish woman to complete this swim. I had persevered despite my fear and insecure feelings.

This out of comfort zone experience proved to me again that I can do more than I think. I took the risk of failure. I faced this

.allenge completely alone without my trusted friends, whom I have known for years, family, or colleagues. I believe the universe created, in a short time, my social support environment to help me. It was great that Kumar was with me for support. It was the first time when I didn't have any expectations from my trusted environment for support. I was ready to face this challenge alone, but I was more surprised when he said that he wanted to

support me and was planning to write a book from the inspiration he felt from my journey. Ryan swam with me, Monene Murray, a consultant, coach, and a passioned cold water swimmer from South Africa, whom I had met in Turkey, gave me some valuable hints and swam with me the day before. All the good things and people came together, and in the end, all turned out well.

SUMMARY

1. **Always follow our passion.** Your brain is your limit.
2. **Break your comfort zone and your limiting beliefs**. Expand your comfort zone, reduce your fear zone, and explore yourself. Take the risk of failing. You are more than you think!
3. **Get stronger!** Desire, determination, and taking risks despite the possibility of failing, make you stronger, and push your growth zone.

16

Lockdown in South Africa – Covid 19

After the Robben Island swim, I flew back from Cape Town to Johannesburg. At the airport, I saw more than ever health and safety regulations. Everybody had a mask, and you could see hand sanitizers everywhere. Covid 19 was a worldwide topic, but for me, it felt so far away in South Africa.

The global pandemic of Coronavirus disease 2019 (COVID-19) was first reported on 31 December 2019 by the World Health Organization following a cluster of pneumonia cases in Wuhan City, Hubei Province of China. Severe acute respiratory syndrome Coronavirus 2 (SARS-CoV-2) has been confirmed as the causative virus of COVID-19. To date, COVID-19 has become a global pandemic, and it is continuing to spread across the globe.

These were the facts, but now, it was also the reality for us. Corona cases appeared in South Africa as well. Within three weeks, all restaurants had been closed, the clubhouse in my complex closed, the gym closed, the pool closed, the shops closed, the office closed – so everything that I enjoyed with people in Johannesburg had been closed.

The virus we were fighting against was forcing all of us to stay at home. That meant no more socializing activities, no swimming, no going out for a run. There were five levels of lockdown. For the first 35 days, we were in level 5 and not even allowed to go for a walk inside our complex or buy alcohol. The highlight of the day for me was to go out in my complex to have a short walk to the trash bins. In level 4, we were allowed to run from 6 to 9 am. We were only allowed to go out for essential purchases, such as buying food or getting medical treatments. Alcohol, cigarettes, anything deemed unessential, was forbidden. After 7 pm, there was a curfew. In Level 3, we were allowed to run without time constraints and had no curfew after 7 pm. If I were in Cape Town, maybe I could have walked on the beach or even swum, but here in Johannesburg, the places to walk, swim, and run were limited.

Staying at home was the best thing that we could do for ourselves and for our fellow human beings to prevent the spread of Covid-19. The measures showed their effectiveness, and the disease started to come under control. But this lockdown turned out to be another out of comfort zone experience for me.

Everybody would agree with me that our home is our ideal comfort area. Isn't it? Ideally, it should be. I would never imagine that I was reflecting about staying at home as an out of comfort zone experience.

My home has always been my comfort zone, where I can find time and my space to rest, to regenerate and to distance myself for some time from all the business and social life. A place where I regain my deepest energy to get myself ready to go out again, socialize, work, work out, and have some out of comfort zone experiences for individual and professional growth.

Naturally, we are social animals. Across all cultures, races, ages, and genders, humans have basic needs for social and emotional connection. We also have a need for balance.

During this lockdown, we were limiting ourselves from being near our loved ones or going outside. Some people may have lost their jobs, and some may have kids at home and trying to work productively while taking care of their babies.

Some may have some relationship issues…stuck at home, trying to figure relationship problems out and still trying to perform for the outside world.

Some could be completely alone, and some could be a sport and nature addict like me and can't train properly in nature.

All those limitations were challenges for all of us, which demonstrate my definition of an out of comfort zone experience as well.

We took so many things for granted. Our freedom, our health, our loved ones next to us, walking on the street, working with our colleagues and having breaks together, dining with friends, drinking a glass of wine, and much more. Who could imagine that even swimming would be forbidden?

I had not been swimming for more than three months for the first time in my life, sitting completely alone in Johannesburg far away from my family and friends.

When we moved to Level 4, I ran every morning around 8 to 10 kilometers and started doing cross-fit to strengthen my overall body and keep activating my muscles. Because of running, I started feeling a pain in my ankle, which was operated in January, again. Life was testing our patience in different areas, and the art was trying to stay optimistic and being grateful for everything we still have in our lives – especially our own mental and physical health. I decided to try new hobbies and started with horse riding and tennis lessons. This experience provided me with new dimensions in my life and showed me that there are always surprises in life. We just need to embrace life.

THE PLANS CAN CHANGE, AND FLEXIBILITY IS KEY IN LIFE.

I had planned so many trips in South Africa. My German friends, Theresa and Andreas, with whom I had swum in Munich Eisbach, wanted to visit me. We were planning to go to the Garden Route, which is a famous and beautiful 300-kilometer (190 miles) road on the south-western coast of South Africa, extending from Witsand in the Western Cape to the border of Tsitsikamma Storms River in the Eastern Cape. I wanted to go to Mozambique and take a dolphin boat tour with my friend, Tarbi. I wanted to go to Cape Town again to hike with Ryan to Table Mountain. I even wanted to fly to Mauritius and enjoy the sun and the sea. All these plans ended. Moreover, I had registered for a slot to swim around Manhattan Island in the Hudson River, New York, which is around 42 km and would have been my first long solo swim. I also wanted to swim the Catalina Channel between Santa Catalina Island and the Palos Verdes Peninsula in California. Needless to say, all plans were canceled. I needed to accept it, respect it, and just follow the flow, trying to be flexible and staying optimistic.

COHERENT HEART AND COHERENT MIND WITH MEDITATION – ACCESSING THE HEART'S INTELLIGENCE

When people describe me, they would say that I am always on the move. I always need to do something and can't stay in one place for long. This is very true. But this lockdown taught me that I can stay in one place, and I can even live without swimming or my trusted environment. I am more than what I thought I could handle. In addition to my cross-fit workout exercises, meditation helped me a lot.

I started with the meditation led by Dr. Joe Dispenza, an international lecturer, researcher, corporate consultant, author, and educator, who has been invited to speak in more than 32 countries on five continents. During the lockdown, he offered a free 10-day course, and I attended every second. The combination of lockdown and meditation changed my life. I could go to a deeper level in my mind, could connect the right and left hemispheres of my brain at the same time with my heart. I try to do this medi-ation every morning, and I feel more and more my real purpose in life.

Dr. Joe Dispenza describes his method in his website (https://blog.drjoedispenza.com/blog/heart/accessing-the-hearts-intelligence) in the article on accessing the hearts intelligence like this:

"Since 2013, we've gone to great lengths to measure and quantify coherence and transformation, and central to both coherence and transformation is understanding the heart's role. Almost every-one knows the elevated feelings of the heart—love, compassion, gratitude, joy, unity, and so on. These are feelings that fill us up and make us feel wholeness, connectedness, and oneness, rather the feelings of stress that divide communities and drain individuals of vital energy. The problem is that often the elevated feelings of the heart occur through chance—dependent upon something external in our environment—rather than something we can produce on demand. What we've found in studying the many facets of the heart, however, is that, in fact, we can regulate our internal states, independent of the conditions in our external environment. Just like developing any skill, it requires knowledge and practice.

We know that in order to create a new future, a person needs to marry a clear intention (coherent brain) with an elevated emotion (coherent heart). With the intention or thought acting as the electrical charge, and the feeling or emotion acting as a magnetic charge, this is how we change our energy—and when we change our energy, we change our life. It's the communion of these two ingredients that begin to produce a clear effect on matter by moving our biology from living in the past to living in the future. Only then can we cease being a victim of circumstance and begin living as a creator of our reality. This is the process whereby we create a new personal reality."

This meditation doesn't take long, just 30 minutes, and the impact is huge. You can do it in your daily life as well. As Dr. Joe Dispenza explains: "Simply find a quiet moment in your day and find stillness in your body and mind by paying attention to your breathing. Each time you take a breath, slow it down, place your awareness where your heart is, then practice cultivating those heightened, elevated emotions that connect us to everyone and everything. Just as we unconsciously cultivate fear, jealousy, anger, or sadness on a regular basis, if we practice feeling elevated emotions every day, who knows—it might just become how we normally feel. When our heart is open, we are more intuitive, more patient, more connected, more present, more forgiving, and more knowing. That's why I like to say the brain thinks, but the heart knows."

The sun will rise again soon. The night is darkest just before dawn...

For what can you be grateful? The sun will rise every day. Every time, when we feel the darkness, don't forget that sunshine will appear in the morning again. I believe in the Ying and Yang philosophy.

According to the book *Religions in the Modern World: Traditions and Transformations* by Linda Woodhead, Christopher Partridge, and Hiroko Kawanami - 2016, in Chinese cosmology, the universe creates itself out of a primary chaos of material energy, organized into the cycles of Yin and Yang and formed into objects and lives. Yin is the receptive and Yang the active principle, seen in all forms of change and difference, such as the annual cycle (winter and summer), the landscape (north-facing shade and south-facing brightness), sexual coupling (female and male), the formation of both women and men as characters, and sociopolitical history (disorder and order). Darkness and sunlight, happiness, and sadness are also in the same cycle. Without sadness, we can't appreciate our happiness, without being alone, we can't appreciate others' company and love, without feeling pain, we cannot feel comfort and gratefulness. This period showed me this, and I even started appreciating the pain. Because even with pain, we are growing.

I started to write this book during the lockdown. Maybe, without this extraordinary situation, I would have procrastinated on the idea of writing a book. I was also able to reflect on what I wanted more of in my life, and less. This period has given us the opportunity to reflect, grow, and be grateful for what we have in life.

With every new experience, you explore yourself and your potential.

BE THANKFUL FOR ALL GOOD AND BAD EXPERIENCES

Without bad experiences, without pain, without failure, you never explore the best right way - your potential, your real thinking way. With every new situation, you explore yourself, you learn about your past experiences about your coping strategies, and you go further step by step. There is no backward step. Life is continuing; you are growing with all your good and bad experiences. Accept those, love those, and enjoy your growth!

My challenging swimming experiences, family life, and lockdown experience in South Africa gave me the opportunity to step out of my comfort zone and grow both mentally and physically. Our life journey defines us, but we define our life journey as well. Always remember that you have the power; you are more than you think, never give up. Always follow your dreams and passion. Even if you have failures or bad experiences in life, be thankful for them. Each experience will provide you with a better self on your journey, and you will transform day by day.

SUMMARY

1. **Don't take things for granted.** Your freedom, your health, your loved ones next to you, walking on the street, working with your colleagues and having breaks together, dining with friends, drinking a glass of wine, and much more. Appreciate everything that you have in life.

2. **The plans can change, always be flexible, and try to make the most of the situation.** Accept what's happening and what's not in your control. Respect it, and just follow the flow, try to stay optimistic and protect your healthy mood.

3. **Coherent heart and coherent brain with Meditation - Accessing the Heart's Intelligence**

4. **Meditation helps you to calm down and reflect on what you really want in your life. It helps you to connect with your soul in hard times.** To create a new future, a person needs to marry a clear intention (coherent brain) with an elevated emotion (coherent heart). With the intention or thought acting as the electrical charge, and the feeling or emotion acting as a magnetic charge, this is how we change our energy - and when we change our energy, we change our life.

5. **Never forget: The night is darkest just before dawn**. Every time you feel sad or bad, motivate yourself with this mindset. It can't be worse, and you will get stronger and stronger. Without sadness, we can't appreciate our happiness, without being alone, we can't appreciate others' company and love, without feeling pain, we cannot feel comfort and gratefulness.

6. **Be thankful for all good and bad experiences.** Without bad experiences, without pain, without failure, you never explore the best right way – your potential, your real thinking way. With every new situation, you explore yourself, you learn about your past experiences, about your coping strategies, and you go further step by step. There is no backward step. Life is a continuum.

17

Life is short, and Corona was real

I was in Datça, my favorite place during the summer vacations, and everything was fine until I found out that my father had Covid. He had already been fighting cancer for 4 years and always managed to stay strong. As my father had been vaccinated, I didn't take it too seriously at first and wished him all the best for a speedy recovery.

On the last day of my vacation, my father's wife called me and said that my father had woken up very late and had a fever. He tried to get on the phone but couldn't speak and had difficulty getting to the next room. He was in a critical condition. I immediately called the ambulance and sent the doctors to their home.

Day 1, day 2, day 3 ... I tried to reach him, to visit him, but I couldn't ... The doctors wouldn't allow me to see him. I couldn't even speak to my father properly. My half-sister bought him a sim card, a cell phone, but she still couldn't talk to him.

I was already planning to move to Switzerland before his illness, and he knew it.

After a few days, I finally managed to hear his voice. The last time we spoke, and I didn't know it would be the last time, my father asked, "Are you going to move to Switzerland?" With mixed feelings, I gave a short and uncomfortable answer, "I think so." That was our last brief conversation. From that day on, everything passed at a pace I could no longer control.

The days went by, the doctors' conversations became less and less encouraging, and I felt so helpless, and sad. One day, the doctor called me and told me that my father had to be intubated, that he could no longer breathe and that the treatments were not working. I went to the hospital and wanted to say goodbye to my father before he fell asleep. They let me see him. It was hard to see him suffer; he couldn't breathe; he couldn't look me in the eye; he couldn't talk to me.

I can't tell you how sad and helpless I felt in those moments. Of course, he felt me and my support. I was the only one who visited him and made the decision about his treatment. I didn't want to accept that his condition was deteriorating. I felt that I had a difficult role in making decisions and taking responsibility for his treatment.

After a few days, the doctors asked me to stop the treatment process because his condition was deteriorating. There was no chance of recovery. The treatment was aimed at keeping him alive for longer. His kidneys were failing, his organs were no longer functioning, and with all the treatments, he could barely stay awake. I didn't want to believe it; I didn't want to accept it and just wanted the maximum treatment to continue. Nothing helped; the doctors did everything they could. During this time, I constantly feared receiving bad news on the phone.

He finally decided to leave the universe of his own accord. The doctor called me and said I could see him before he died. Immediately after the phone call, I left the house, picked up my mother from the airport and took her to the hospital. Although they had separated more than twenty years ago, my mother came to the hospital to support me, and we experienced the most difficult minutes of our lives. Somehow, I felt pure love and the deepest pain.

I held his hand, stroked his head, and repeated out loud how much I loved him.

His heartbeat accelerated while I became more and more emotional. After a few minutes, I let it all go and accepted the situation. I prayed, held his hand, and sent him my energy and pure love. His heartbeat became slower and slower.

50 ... 40 ... 35 ... 27 ...

15 ... 10 ... 8 ...

4 ... 0 ... moment of silence ... moment of acceptance ... moment of confrontation with reality ...

0 MOMENT OF SILENCE AND ACCEPTANCE

Sometimes, we have to step out of our comfort zone. This is not always our own decision. Sometimes, we find ourselves in situations where we have no choice and can't control everything that happens around us. All we can do in these situations is accept what is happening, trust the universe and control how we remedy, think and deal with our feelings.

The past few days - and especially this moment of silence - have taught me to accept what has happened and to let it all go. I have said goodbye to my father, the man I loved the most in my life. He will always live in my heart. I'm learning to accept what I can't control and let it flow with love and peace. We grow up with pain and sorrow.

Always cherish every moment, the time you spend with your loved ones. Life is too short.

Farewell, Dad. I will always love you.

Your daughter,

Deniz

SUMMARY

1. **Life is short; we should cherish every moment and enjoy life to the fullest!** This may sound banal or normal to you, but I really mean it! Stop worrying about tomorrow! Problems or difficult situations will come anyway, whether you worry about them or not. Just like the good things in your life. No matter what you think and do, good or bad things will happen in your life. If something is meant to happen, it will happen. You can't control everything in life. You can accept what happens and control your reactions, emotions, and efforts to make things better so that you feel better. Stop worrying, just be grateful, accept and live the moment to the fullest! Always cherish every moment, the time you spend with your loved ones! Life is too short.

2. **We grow up with pain and sorrow.** The extraordinary thing is that each of us has the ability to re-create and re-emerge. Perhaps the true purpose of suffering is for us to rise out of our pain, to evolve, grow and achieve (quote from Judy Tatelbaum, American writer and therapist, from "Embrace Life after Loss" by Allen Klein).

3. **Transform pain into creative energy and be the best version of yourself!** Do something good for yourself first and then for others. The better you feel about yourself, the better you can behave towards others.

18

The extreme level of individual transformation – magic happens outside the comfort zone! World Ice Swimming Championships

YOU NEVER KNOW WHAT YOU CAN ACHIEVE OUTSIDE YOUR COMFORT ZONE

On this trip, the universe showed me that you can achieve more than you can imagine and that you can go beyond your limits. I have always wanted to work and live by a lake or the sea, swim in the water or do visionary things that no Turkish woman has ever done before.

OUTSIDE THE COMFORT ZONE MAGIC HAPPENED AGAIN – I COULDN'T KEEP UP WITH MY OWN PACE.

One evening, Hamza Bakırcıoğlu, the world record holder who had swum 3,450 meters in 1.08 hours in ice-cold water at 4.1 degrees Celsius, called and asked me if I would join the ice swimming committee in Germany and support the preparations for the Ice Swimming World Championships. I agreed, not knowing what to expect and with no expectations. The next day, he asked me if I wanted to join him at the World Championships, represent Turkey and be the first woman in Turkish history to compete at the World Championships. I was very surprised and excited about this opportunity. Everything happened step by step – my move to Switzerland, my training in the cold Lake Zurich, my participation in the Ice Swimming World Championships.

Sie trotzt eisigen Temperaturen und Weissen Haien

Extremschwimmerin aus Männedorf Deniz Kayadelen schwamm schon im Ärmelkanal und von Irland nach Schottland. Für ihr nächstes Abenteuer trainiert sie im eiskalten Zürichsee.

Christian Dietz-Saluz

«Nein, das ist kein Künstlername», sagt Deniz Kayadelen mit entwaffnendem Lächeln. «So heisse ich wirklich.» Deniz bedeutet nämlich auf Türkisch «Meer». Bei ihr wird der Name zur Passion. Denn die in Frankfurt am Main geborene Wirtschaftspsychologin und Senior Managerin eines der weltgrössten Wirtschaftsprüfer ist mit keinem anderen Element so vertraut wie mit dem Wasser – vor allem Meerwasser.

Eine eigene Faustregel

Zürichsee-Zeitung, Switzerland

ICE SWIMMING: AN UNCOMFORTABLE PLACE IS EXTREME

Since I moved to Switzerland and now live directly on Lake Zurich, I've had no excuses not to train in the lake or in the Allgäu, which is only 150 km from Zurich.

DAY 1: ICE CAMP IN THE ALLGAU, GERMANY:

We took to the icy waters with Hamza Bakırcıoğlu, his wonderful wife Dilek, and his father Seyfi because extreme sports like this require strong teamwork. We had a challenging plan for day 1. We had planned to go into the ice-cold water three times – three times in one day!

- Round 1, Sonthofener See: 9 minutes in 6-degree cold water
- Round 2, upstream on the river: 5 minutes in 4.8-degree cold water
- Round 3, in the river: 4 minutes at 4 degrees water temperature

TOGETHER WE ARE STRONGER!

The support system is just as important as the training and mental preparation. Especially after ice swimming, there is a period of shivering, and it takes a while to feel your hands and feet again. Getting my clothes on was a big challenge. Dilek helped me get dressed, and Hamza's father cooked the best soup to warm me up. I was very lucky to be trained by a world record holder and the best ice swimming colleague. Hamza and his family supported me to swim three times in three different places in the winter wonderland. It was a magical moment; such is the flow.

We have the power to control our minds and our body. We create the pain mainly in our minds. It's all a question of attitude and perception. You can do more than you think! You are more than you think. Wellness starts in our head.

Day 2: 9 minutes in 3.2-degree cold water
Day 3: 10 minutes in 3.4-degree cold water

Peter Brönnimann contacted me from an ice swimming group in Stäfa "Eisbären Stäfa" and I started to train with them at the weekends, and on weekdays I trained alone with a safety buoy. A safety buoy is particularly important when you are alone in the water. You never know how your body will react to ice-cold water; it depends on your mood, tiredness, etc. Sometimes, it was difficult to wake up early in the morning in the dark and motivate myself to go into the water, but after the training, I was proud of myself because I had overcome my fears and inner blocks and was encouraged to keep going.

Because of the Coronavirus restrictions, there was a lot of uncertainty about the World Cup, but something told me that it would happen and that we would fly to Glogow, Poland.

The water in Lake Zurich was around 5 to 6 degrees Celsius, and I had to get used to the icy water below 5 degrees Celsius. So, I decided to go back to the Allgäu for a weekend to train with Hamza. We swam 500 meters together, and that gave me the confidence to take part in the 500 meter ice swim in Glogow.

I had confidence, some fear, and mixed feelings. I was very focused on this journey and led a disciplined lifestyle. I paid attention to my sleep, my diet and meditated a lot.

In the last few days before the race, I got increasingly nervous and even started doing night hypnosis and sleep meditations to help calm my mind in addition to the Wim Hof breathing exercises and daily meditations. Twelve months ago, I couldn't even imagine swimming in ice water for more than 3 minutes, let alone moving to Switzerland and preparing for the Ice Swimming World Championships on Lake Zurich. Everything has evolved. After training hard, both mentally and physically, I was ready to take part in the World Championships with mixed feelings of excitement, gratitude, and nervousness of the unknown.

50, 100, 250, 500 meter freestyle and 50 meter butterfly were waiting for me.

WORLD CHAMPIONSHIPS IN GLOGOW, POLAND

The IISA, International Ice Swimming Association, organized the 4th World Championships in Glogow. At the International Ice Swim Association swimming is unassisted in water temperatures below 5.0°C, wearing a silicone swim cap, goggles, and a standard swimsuit. The IISA has set itself the task of including ice swimming as one of the official disciplines in the Winter Olympics.

When we arrived in Poland, we went straight to the swimming pool. I wanted to swim 500 meters to calm down and relax a bit before the race. I wanted to show myself that I could get through this distance without any physical complications. I panicked a little during the training, and my heart rate increased. I was afraid of that, but I was well prepared and hoped everything would go well.

The water was around 3.2 degrees. They had built a 25-meter-long pool in the stream. The competitions were to start in the pool, and no somersaults were allowed.

There were 300 swimmers from 30 countries present. It was great to experience this atmosphere. Despite the cold, I was able to savor these moments.

DAY 1: 500-METER BUTTERFLY – I SURVIVED, AND EVEN MORE, I BECAME WORLD CHAMPION!

On the first day, I swam 500 meters; the hardest race was the first on day 1. Hamza came with me to the swimming area to support me, count the laps and give me a signal after 450 meters. In that cold water, you feel like your brain is frozen and you can't count anymore, so it's good to have someone looking after you and supporting you from the outside to motivate and protect you.

There were observers, medical staff, and divers for each lane. The safety precautions were really high, and I felt comfortable and safe in this environment.

Five hundred meters to the start: The observer signals, "Take off your clothes. Go into the water." And the starting tone went "beep." In long races like this, controlling your pace and body temperature is very important. If you start too fast, you lose heat quickly; if you start too slowly, you lose the race. I swam carefully for the first 100 meters, didn't sprint, and tried to control my body and mind. After 200 meters, I could no longer feel my hands and feet. The turns became more and more difficult. You had to touch the wall at every turn, and I could no longer feel the wall. I lost a lot of time in the turns to avoid a possible disqualification, and somehow, I made sure I touched the wall. My hands were like a board, not part of my body. It was a strange feeling. At the same time, I felt adrenaline, excitement, and the desire to finish the course with my best performance. In the last 50 meters, Hamza gave me the special signal, and I tried to swim faster. In the last 25 meters, I saw another swimmer next to me and wanted to be faster than him. Then I realized that he still had 50 meters to swim, and I came second in the mixed-age group in that event. When I wanted to get out, I could no longer feel my hands and couldn't take off my swimming cap. I was very relieved to have finished the course. I was happy about my participation and the fact that I was the first Turkish woman to participate in the World Ice Swimming Championships. I would have automatically set all Turkish records. However I was curious about my overall performance and waited for the medals to be awarded.

After a few hours of waiting, the ceremony began. I was expecting a medal in the 30 to 34 age group, but I ended up in the 35 to 39 category. And what suddenly happened?

The presenter called my name in an excited voice: "And the winners ... And the world champion over 500 meters, Deniz Kayadelen!"

I couldn't believe that I was the world champion over 500 meters in my age group. It was truly magical.

DAY 2: 100 METRES FREESTYLE – 1 SILVER MEDAL

I swam 100 metres freestyle. It was a relaxed day compared to the day before. I met really nice people, spent time with them, watched other swimmers and mentally prepared myself for the last day. I came second in that race and won the silver medal. I was happy again, but it was nothing compared to the excitement of the first day.

DAY 3: 3 RACES IN ONE DAY – 2 GOLD MEDALS AND 1 SILVER MEDAL

My day started with 250 meters. That was another new experience for me. It wasn't short enough to swim a sprint straight away, but also not long enough to start very slowly. Compared to day 1, I was more relaxed and just let it go.

The 250 meters went well. Afterwards, I went into the hot tub to warm up after the cold. There was also a sauna, and I tried to warm up and prepare for the next race. I took an hour's break to warm up, dry off and get ready again.

The water in the warm water pool stank, but that didn't bother anyone because the main thing was to warm up, not to have a clean water experience.

After drinking a hot chocolate and fortifying myself, I continued with the 50 metre butterfly race. It was very hard to feel the water, and I immediately tried to swim a sprint. It was a completely different feeling compared to a normal swimming race. It's very difficult to start a sprint when your mind is panicking in the cold, your breathing is restricted, and your muscles just want to feel the warm water. It's all a question of attitude and hard work. After the 50 metre butterfly, I went back into the warm water pool and had to wait 20 minutes for the last race – the 50 metre freestyle. I enjoyed the warm water, chatted to the other swimmers, and tried to concentrate on the next final heat.

It was windy and cold outside. I got out of the water with a wet body and went straight to registration. My name was called, and I went to the final race with wet and shaking hands. It was really hard to warm up my body and concentrate. I accepted the situation and tried to do my best. I felt the wind and the cold in all my pores, and when I went back into the water, I felt the icy cold to the full, but I said to myself: "Come on, you can do it this last time..." There was no chance of a controlled start in those 50 meters. I had to sprint the whole way. I tried to swim a sprint after the start and gave it my best shot. Compared to a normal swimming pool, it was completely different this time, and that was normal. No turning, no conventional jumps from the edge, only a chilling plunge into water measuring a mere 3 degrees Celsius, a stark departure from the usual pool temperature of 24 degrees.

When I think about what it was like to get into the cold water, I realize that a gradual change has taken place. The cold has taught me a lot on this journey: Focus, concentration, dealing with my fears and much more.

Aus der Angst vor dem Eiswasser wurden drei Weltmeistertitel

Eisschwimmerin aus Männedorf Dreimal Gold, zweimal Silber nach Männedorf: Auch wenn das keine olympische Bilanz aus Peking, sondern von der Eisschwimm-WM in Polen ist, glänzen die Medaillen.

[illegible]

«Das Wasser war 3,2 Grad, ich bin da fast mit Todesangst zum Rennen über die 500 Meter Freistil hineingestiegen.»

[illegible]

LAKE ZURICH SWISS NEWSPAPER

In short, I survived! 💪

It was a great activity and a unique ice experience. I received so many messages from all over the world, and I am so grateful for the support and good energy I received from everyone.

My journey into cold water began 15 years ago with hypothermia in 17-degree water. I hated cold water and loved hot showers.

Three years ago, despite my great fear of cold water, I started cold water training and Wim Hof's breathing technique for the relay races in the English Channel and the North Channel. The cold has changed my life - I have learned to control my mind and body and to concentrate better.

Two years ago, despite my fear of sharks, I decided to swim from Robben Island to Cape Town and swam for about two hours in the cold Atlantic water. I also started meditating to get a grip on my fears and gain control over my body, mind, and soul.

A year ago, I couldn't even imagine staying in ice water for more than 3 minutes. I was inspired by others, set myself small challenges and started a real training session on Lake Zurich 3 months ago.

😱 In the last three days, I had competed in 5 races at the IISA World Championships 2022, and today, I was on my way back with 3 gold and 2 silver medals.

A summary of these days:

🏆 500m freestyle gold

🏆 250m freestyle gold

🥈 100m freestyle silver

🥈 50m freestyle silver

🏆 50m butterfly gold

♡ Friendship with first-class people who
show real resilience and strength 🙏

👄 Inspiration for the path ahead: My limit is my imagination. Despite your fears and inner barriers, follow your dream, follow your passion, work hard, take time for your conscious renewal, and believe in yourself! Even if your mind tells you otherwise and your feelings express themselves in the form of fear. You are more than you think, and you will be surprised at what you are really capable of!

19

Fear is your best friend – Preparing for the ultimate goal

A weekend in Basel at Dr. Joe Dispenza's seminar, an intense meditation with more than 3000 people in the room, and I saw myself crossing the English Channel alone... It felt so real. I had made a connection with my future, and the connection became real. After that seminar, I called my coach and told him the time had come. I was ready to walk the walk – to cross the English Channel solo. I don't know how or if I could do it, but I was actively going to give it a go. I asked him to secure a slot for me, and the intense preparation journey began.

In meditation, we let go of our fears and our egos, and suddenly, I saw many things crystal clear.

I have realized that fear acts like a compass that shows me the way to personal growth and change. It shows me what my desires are when it doesn't exist. It sparks creativity and makes life much more vibrant. Imagine a life without fear – how boring that would be! If you had no fear, what changes would you make today? What would you start doing? This question alone can open new perspectives in your mind.

Paradoxically, fear is both your obstacle and your greatest ally. Even though fear may seem like a closed door, but it is actually an open one. If you walk through this door, you can achieve more than you ever thought possible.

Remember: the more you venture beyond your comfort zone, the more self-confidence you gain. You expand your comfort zone, challenge your inner limits, and activate your learning and growth zones. Conquering the unknown empowers you to do great things.

When I discovered the strength to venture beyond my comfort zone, I began to dream bigger and muster the courage to take on even greater challenges. If someone had told me three years ago that I would one day become an ice swimmer, let alone a world champion, I would have laughed. Me, an ice swimmer? After my battle with hypothermia and my aversion to the cold, it seemed completely unlikely.

Did you know that everyone is born with only two innate fears: the fear of falling and the fear of loud noises? All other fears are learned or acquired, such as the fear of failure, inadequacy, pain, or rejection. Our life experiences and our environment shape these fears and often limit us.

The reason why many of us don't pursue our dreams lies in our minds. Our limiting beliefs and fears create barriers that keep us trapped in the safety of our comfort zone.

FINALLY REALIZING MY CHILDHOOD DREAM: SWIMMING SOLO ACROSS THE ENGLISH CHANNEL

Preparing for the Channel crossing was already a long journey. I underwent rigorous training in cold conditions, put on weight to better endure the cold water and mentally prepared myself for a grueling 15-hour non-stop swim. I flew to Turkey in winter to train in 15 to 17 degrees. I flew to Dover to train in 14 to 15 degrees. I was always looking for the right water temperatures to prepare myself. When the lakes in Switzerland got warmer in the summer, I even went to mountain lakes and constantly looked for the right conditions. It was a huge investment of time, money and, above all, energy.

COLD-WATER LONG-DISTANCE SWIMMING CAMP IN MENORCA

To qualify for the solo swim in the English Channel, you have to demonstrate the ability to swim continuously for six hours in water below 15 degrees Celsius.

I traveled to Barcelona and then to Menorca, a tranquil and enchanting island. This swim camp was organized by Kings Swimmers and led by Kevin Murphy, the true authority of the Channel. He can claim to have completed more Channel swims than anyone else, an achievement recognized by the Channel Swimming Association. The title and the prestigious Letona Trophy are currently held by Kevin Murphy, who swam the Channel 34 times between 1968 and 2006.

DAY 1: ARRIVAL AND ACCLIMATIZATION

We checked into a comfortable hotel with spacious apartments on the first day. I shared an apartment with another swimmer; we each had our own room but shared the kitchen. At 4 pm we gathered at the hotel for a safety briefing and introduced ourselves to each other. We then went swimming in the bay to acclimatize and were divided into groups according to our swimming ability.

DAY 2: SETTLING IN

We spent the day in the water getting used to our surroundings and making friends with the swimmers in our group. We swam for a total of 4 hours, with a break in between. There was also an evening session and an optional night swim, which was canceled due to the stormy weather. During these 2 hours of swimming, I felt considerable discomfort in my hips due to a persistent hip flexion problem. In the cold water, I felt a blockage after about 45 minutes, followed by severe pain after 60 minutes, which was quite demotivating.

DAY 3: BUILDING UP ENDURANCE

That day, we swam for a total of 5 hours in 15-degree water, with a one-hour break in between. In the early evening, we had a seminar led by Kevin Murphy.

DAY 4: THE CRITICAL 6-HOUR SWIM AND THE PAINFUL DEFEAT

This day was crucial for me as I had to complete a 6-hour coastal swim to qualify for a solo crossing of the English Channel. Three boats awaited us on the shore: one for the fastest swimmers, one for the slowest and one in the middle with all the necessary supplies. I was nervous and worried about the cold and my ongoing hip flexion problems. I was aware of the importance of this swim for my qualification and was determined to make it.

After 2 hours, I realized that 60% of the swimmers had already left the water. I could feel my pace slowing down; the cold was setting in, and the water was getting choppy and rough. Despite this, I remained focused and determined to complete the qualification. After 3 hours and during a refreshment break, I started to shiver, and the crew suggested I leave the water. I insisted that I was fine and swam on but noticed that the boat in the slowest group was next to me, while the fastest group I had started with was 500 meters ahead of me and getting further away. I felt deeply demoralized.

After 3.5 hours, the crew decided to pull me out as they noticed that my speech was slowing down, indicating the onset of hypothermia. The strong current made it impossible for me to make any progress; my arm movements were no match for the force of the current. It was a disheartening experience, and I couldn't help but feel frustrated and pressured, especially after 15 years of cold weather training, including ice swimming, to be faced with hypothermia again.

DAY 5: REGENERATION – BUILDING HOPE AND STRENGTH

"Finding Inner Peace"

I swam for just an hour and then sought advice from my spiritual coach Faine. During our hour-long session, we talked about my fears, my thoughts, my pain, and the time pressures of being a full-time counselor. Faine reiterated a powerful message: inner peace and stopping my thoughts would allow me to enjoy swimming. She emphasized that my body would protect me and that the universe was on my side. My brain, with its incessant thoughts, was the source of pain, stress, and diminished energy. It distracted me from being in the moment and focusing on one swim stroke at a time. We did a long meditation session where I found my inner peace, embraced the moment, tapped into the energy of my soul, and felt a deep sense of calm.

DAY 6: A SECOND CHANCE TO QUALIFY

This time, we stayed close to the hotel on a quiet beach. There was another swimmer in our group with a similar pace, and I decided to swim the full 6 hours alongside him. Together, we were stronger. It worked like a charm. We started together and made eye contact every three strokes, took a breath, and kept going. I adjusted my technique to alleviate my hip flexion issues, and that helped. After 3 hours, I took a few pain pills, but overall, I felt calmer, more focused on the moment and determined to finish.

I started to shake again at the 4-hour mark, but the knowledge that I had completed over 50% of the swim gave me inner strength. With the sun shining brightly, I motivated myself, kept up my pace and swam alongside my partner. After 5 hours,

I knew I had it in the bag. I enjoyed the last few minutes and dreamt of a hot shower and delicious Chinese food.

Six hours in 14.8-degree water - mission accomplished! I felt an overwhelming mixture of happiness, pride, exhaustion, and a sense of achievement.

After this exciting and challenging day, we gathered for a delicious dinner followed by a certification ceremony.

DAY 7: FAREWELL SWIM WITH PRIDE AND JOY

We had one last one-hour swim with my swimming friends on our last day. It was a relaxed swim accompanied by warm smiles. After the swim, I enjoyed a warm shower and then drove back to my work in Zurich with the triumphant memories of this remarkable trip.

Despite successfully completing the camp and gaining my qualifications, I still struggled with lingering fears and limiting beliefs. However, my desire to realize my dream surpassed these obstacles. I realized it is better to try something and possibly fail than not try at all and be trapped in your fears.

THE LAST 6 WEEKS – FEAR STILL THERE?

As I only had 6 to 8 weeks left, my nervousness increased, and the fear was still running through me. This emotional state was difficult to cope with, sapped my energy and tested my courage. I had done everything I could to prepare for this big challenge: many hours of training, cold water camps, daily workouts, cancelling social invitations, prioritizing recovery, chiropractic care for my muscles, physical therapy for my hip joints, and meditation and visualization exercises. I was willing to do whatever it took, using every method available to make my dream a reality, and I had to say no to a lot of things to get closer to my dream.

One day, I decided to see a hypnotherapist. Despite my efforts to control my mind and body, I realized that my subconscious thoughts remained untouched and needed to be addressed and trained for this challenge. I found a competent hypnotherapist and had three sessions with him. In these sessions, he dealt with my goals, wishes and fears in detail. At the beginning of the session, he asked me a crucial question: What is your goal? What do you want to take away from these sessions?

I explained my goal to him: I wanted to realize my dream, but more than that, I wanted to enjoy every moment of this challenge. I wanted to enjoy it, even in the face of pain and difficulty. My ultimate goal was to silence my thoughts and experience the journey without the burden of fear.

He nodded in understanding and made a plan. The schedule was very tight with only 6 weeks left, but he was committed to helping me get there. Over the course of three sessions, I closed my eyes and engaged in dialogs where he spoke directly to my subconscious. During these sessions, my thought patterns were reprogrammed, and the fears that were holding me back were eliminated.

WHAT CAN SPORTS HYPNOSIS BE USED FOR?

Sports hypnosis is a powerful tool that can be used in various aspects of sports performance to promote mental calm, focus and emotional detachment. Here are some ways in which sports hypnosis can be used:

1. **Improving concentration**

   Sports hypnosis helps athletes concentrate better on the task at hand and eliminate distractions that can impair performance.

2. **Pain management**

   Sports hypnosis teaches athletes effective pain management techniques to overcome discomfort during training and competition.

3. **Dealing with nervousness**

   Sports hypnosis helps to overcome nervousness and performance anxiety so that athletes can remain calm under pressure.

4. **Motivation boost**

   Hypnosis can increase motivation and help athletes to pursue their goals even in difficult situations.

5. **Reduction of performance anxiety**

   Sports hypnosis can reduce performance anxiety, which often results from the fear of failure or external pressure.

6. **Reduction of fears (e.g. fear of hypothermia)**

   Hypnosis can be used specifically to **reduce** fears associated with certain problems, e.g. the fear of hypothermia when swimming in cold water.

Sports hypnosis uses the same techniques as traditional hypnosis but tailors them to the specific demands of sports performance. It focuses on helping athletes achieve mental clarity, stay in the present moment and maintain calm, which is essential for peak performance.

In sports psychology, there are several key categories that relate to an athlete's mindset, including:

1. **Arousal regulation**

   Finding the optimal level of arousal or excitement to perform at your best, neither too relaxed nor too stressed.

2. **Goal setting**

   Set long-term and short-term goals to orient and motivate yourself and break down larger goals into achievable milestones.

3. **Imagery**

   Creating vivid mental images that encompass all sensory experiences to practice skills, remember past successes and visualize desired outcomes.

4. **Pre-performance rituals**

   Establishing routines or actions before the competition to create the right level of excitement and readiness.

5. **Self-talk**

   Cultivating positive and constructive self-talk to boost self-confidence, maintain focus and avoid negative thinking patterns.

The importance of mindset in sports cannot be overstated. The mind profoundly affects the body, and hypnosis provides access to the subconscious mind, which plays an important role in an athlete's overall performance. By addressing challenges and fears, sports hypnosis can help athletes reach their full potential and achieve peak performance.

THE LAST 5 WEEKS

It's hard to believe that it's only 5 weeks until the big day! I'm excited and nervous.

The last three months in figures:

- Gained 6 kg to cope better with the cold
- Swam 380 km in a total of 128 hours
- Out of 380 km, 200 km swam in cold water below 16 degrees
- Swam 3 x 6 hours, swam 5 x 4 hours
- Swam 6 x 3 hours
- Meditated 4 days a week to balance my mind
- 12 hours of physiotherapy to solve my hip flexion problems in cold water
- 20 hours of mental coaching
- 10 chiropractor sessions to relieve tension in my shoulders
- More than 100 motivating conversations with my dear friends, colleagues, family members, customers and even strangers

DOVER, JUNE 2023

You can see my swimming cap in this picture. The slogan reads: "I can, and I will."

Only two weekends were left to work towards my peak. I planned to swim 8 to 10 hours and then slow down, recover, and prepare my mind true to the motto of my swim cap: "I can and I will"

PEAK PERFORMANCE TRAINING –10 HOURS NON-STOP SWIMMING

More than 60% is brain power! I knew that, and before the big swim and before tapering, I had to swim non-stop for 10 hours. The English Channel swim would take more than 10 hours, but I knew that after at least 10 hours of swimming, my brain would be ready for at least 10 to 15 hours of swimming. It was the first time in my life that I had set myself the goal of swimming for 10 hours. Fortunately, my swimming friend Jürgen offered me his help. He has a nice sailing boat and knows the challenge of such a preparation trip. I gratefully accepted his support, and we met early in the morning in Männedorf. I was ready, he was ready, and we set off straight away. I sent him my nutrition plan the day before, and he prepared all the motivational posters for me. Every 20 minutes, he showed me the minutes, and every 45 minutes, he gave me the food we had agreed on. He was so focused and helpful. Train by train, I swam on. Those 10 hours felt so hard, but luckily, the water was more than 19 degrees, about 21 degrees, and the sun was shining. It was a warm water swim, but the duration and endurance were challenging. I wanted to train my brain to deal with my thoughts and boredom.

MY LESSON LEARNED FROM THIS 10-HOUR SWIM:

- The sensation of pain has a limit; after that, it doesn't get any worse. At some point, you get used to it and can deal with it better.
- Even the feeling of boredom doesn't get any worse after a certain point. There is a limit to this feeling, and the brain automatically tries to keep you entertained.
- The negative thoughts will come, but you can easily trick your mind; change the focus with small actions and turn your mind into positivity.
- The recovery time IS 24 hours. The pain in the muscles subsides quickly, and you can still swim with strength the next day if you sleep well and eat a balanced diet.
- It helps to break down the goal! I couldn't even imagine being in the water for 10 hours. I always focused on my next meal and looked forward to it every hour. You can see the goodies in my nutrition plan.

Many thanks to Jürg Hohl for the all-around support and for being the captain of the day! Thank you for managing my food, showing me the time, taking care of the route and the traffic on the lake, and monitoring my mental and physical health from start to finish!

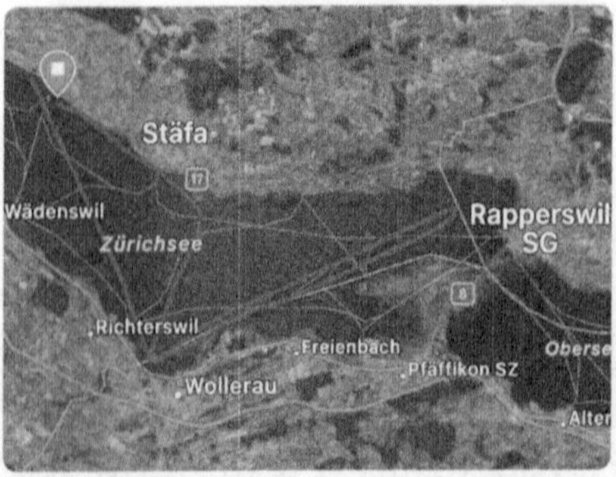

Feeding Swim Plan Deniz 10.06.2023

Time	Feeding	Comment
1st hour	-	
2nd hour	Hot Carb Mix	
3th hour	Hot Carb Mix	If needed painkiller
4th hour	Hot Carb Mix + Energy Gel	If needed extra Magnesium
5th hour	Hot Carb Mix + Banana	
6th hour	Hot Carb Mix + Jelly Babies	If needed painkiller
7th hour	Hot Carb Mix + Freestyle	
8th hour	Hot Carb Mix + Energy Gel	If needed extra motivation push
8 hours 30 min	Hot Carb Mix + Jelly Babies	
9th hour	Hot Carb Mix + Energy Gel	
9 hour 30 min	Hot Carb Mix + Banana	
10th hour	Hot Carb Mix	Finish ☺

Thanks to Ilona Roth for the additional Fitline nutritional support and the motivating dinner before the race. Thanks to Adalvo for the cooperation and the common motto: #alwaysontarget

SUMMARY

1. **Start with small steps and accept the unknown!** I started with just cold-water showers and mental training. Step by step, I then went into the cold water with my support system and expanded my comfort zone.

2. **Even if you feel scared, don't stop dreaming big and believing in yourself!** You don't have to have full self-confidence to achieve your goals. More than 60% of your success depends on your mental strength! Prepare your mind and learn how to overcome your limiting beliefs! Just have the courage to step out of your comfort zone and deal with the uncertainty and pain!

3. **Defeats are part of the journey.** Use these defeats to learn from them and do better next time. Without these experiences, you cannot transform yourself and grow in the long term. Take it for granted, and don't give up!

20

Mount Everest for swimmers – The ultimate self-realization

"DOVERCOASTER" – EMOTIONAL ROLLER COASTER IN DOVER AND THE ATTEMPT TO SWIM ACROSS THE ENGLISH CHANNEL SOLO

The challenge of swimming the English Channel was the culmination of three years of preparation and two decades of dreaming.

Before I left for Dover, my coach called me and said he had bad news for me. Over the next 10 days, the weather seemed to be really terrible, and I would have fourth place, which meant there were 3 swimmers ahead of me. So, if conditions were good, the earliest I could swim was in 4 days, but no one had a chance to swim that far due to the weather conditions. I drove to Dover with this uncertainty. My team was ready and also the ARD documentary team was also ready to film my journey.

TRAING CANCELED – I STARTED PRAYING

Waiting with confidence: Mother Nature is the boss.

As a team, we rented Kevin Murphy's beautiful apartment. My support team arrived, and I got to know everyone: my swimming buddies Yasemin Bagana and Emre Deliveli, and my coach Kamil Resa Alsaran. I shared a room with Jasemin, and we trained every day and waited together for the big day. Day 1, day 2 ... the chances were really slim.

I was so nervous that I fell ill and had a bad case of flu. All the conditions looked so bad. I was literally on a rollercoaster. Now I understand the meaning of Dovercoaster: the emotional roller coaster in Dover!

The weather conditions seemed to be improving, and the first swimmer was already swimming. The second swimmer was too slow, and it was decided to give him another place as it was a time of strong spring tide, which meant that the tide was stronger, and you needed more strength to cope with it. The third swimmer was a lawyer, and it was his turn. Only 2 days to go... If he swam, I wouldn't have a chance to swim. I tried to stay calm and recover from my flu.

I was nervous as I was about to fulfill a lifelong dream. Waiting for suitable swimming conditions was also a test of patience. The possibility of not being able to swim due to unfavorable weather conditions was a given, and I had to overcome a roller coaster of emotions and limiting thoughts to stay calm and hopeful. The incredible support from my team was crucial in keeping a positive attitude.

DAY 5 AND I WAS STILL WAITING

What I have learned so far is to deal with the unknown, trust the process, and trust Mother Nature and the universe, which always has your back! Despite my illness and the uncertainty, I kept meditating, kept listening to my hypnotherapy recordings, kept doing the Wim Hof breathing exercises and kept going to the sauna to recover quickly. I stopped exercising and started praying.

I AM A SOLO CHANNEL SWIMMER!
I AM A CHANNEL SWIMMER!

The big day finally arrived!

The swim in the English Channel was scheduled for July 18. On July 16, the captain gave the go-ahead for the swim, which was due to start at midnight. I immediately got in touch with my spiritual coach Faine Fitzgerald, who was waiting at her sister's house near London for me to start. I also called the documentary film crew, who would be accompanying us. The whole support team felt the intensity of the moment, as swimming the English Channel is often compared to climbing Mount Everest because of its unpredictability for swimmers. The start and finish times are uncertain, and the swim itself presents numerous challenges.

After spending four days in bed, I did a short test swim. The water felt calm, and I felt a sense of peace and readiness. I called my swim doctor to get his clearance to swim with my current health condition as I was battling a lingering flu. He reassured me that my body was up to the challenge and encouraged me to give it a go.

The timing of the swim was as follows:

- I started at 00:36 and swam the first 4 hours in darkness and choppy conditions.

- In the 3rd hour, I started to lose feeling in my hands and feet due to the cold, so I was worried about whether I would last another 10 to 12 hours.
- By the 4th hour, I realized my energy reserves were running low, and I hit my inner wall, which signaled that my carbohydrate reserves were running low, and my body was switching to burning fat for energy.
- At the 10th hour, I had doubts as I swam against the strong current and saw the French coast but I had the feeling I wasn't making any progress. I doubted that I would really reach the shore.

- In the 11th hour I found it difficult to breathe as my nose was blocked and my throat swelled up, making it difficult to breathe without swallowing salt water.
- At the 12th hour, I was able to catch a glimpse of the French coast, and I assumed that I would reach my destination in another hour. Little did I know that the last few kilometers would take another 3 hours.

Despite the exhaustion and challenges, I kept going, determined to reach the shore. The support of my coaches and the belief that I could achieve my dream kept me going. As I approached the final hour, I waited for the arrival of my friend Emre, who would swim the last few meters with me. I saw him getting ready and feeling overwhelming happiness and determination. Together, we set off on the final spurt, and after 15 hours and 16 minutes of uninterrupted swimming, I finally reached the French shore.

The moment I stepped onto the sand was incredible and surreal. I cried, danced, and hugged Emre, overwhelmed with joy. It was a moment of pure happiness and accomplishment. The world seemed to stand still as I danced on the beach and swam back to the boat.

This extraordinary experience felt like a dream come true. Swimming for 15 hours in 16-degree water, surrounded by nature, kissed by jellyfish and dancing with the waves was both surreal and exhilarating. Swimming across the English Channel was not a solo effort but a tremendous team effort and a testament to the power of teamwork and faith.

I have thanked my core team for their mental coaching, emotional support, and technical help. Beyond the immediate team, I have acknowledged the support of family, friends, the swimming community, medical advisors, colleagues, strangers, my hypnotherapist, and my physiotherapist. Their belief and positivity have been instrumental in making this dream a reality.

This journey has shown me how important it is to step out of your comfort zone and confidently pursue your dreams. It has shown that magic can happen with the right preparation, support and belief.

Get out of your comfort zone; magic can happen! Pursue your dreams with confidence!

SUMMARY

1. **Reflect for yourself**: What is your ice water? What is your dream, your purpose, your goal? What would you like to achieve?

2. **Create your own support system**! If I didn't have these great people around me who believe in me and spur me on, I wouldn't be at this stage.

Pain is part of the journey, but it makes you stronger. Pursue your dreams with focus and passion! Don't forget that you are more than your fears and more than you think! Create magic outside your comfort zone!

21

Conclusion – How can you go beyond your limits and get out of your comfort zone?

1. **Trust yourself and use your inner potential!**

   Sometimes, we criticize ourselves too much and live with limiting beliefs: "You can't do it, you're not experienced enough, you don't have the ability, etc." The people around us may also want to protect us and discourage us because of their limiting beliefs. But each of us has our own strengths and potential. Trust yourself first and explore your inner potential by doing new things or doing things differently! Prove to yourself that you can master new challenges! You can do more than you think! I could never have imagined swimming in the North Channel in 12-degree water with poisonous jellyfish and killer whales, but in the end I trusted myself and jumped in.

2. **Think big and start small!**

   Don't be afraid to set high goals and a vision! The limits are your thoughts. Believing in something and thinking big is the first step on the way to your vision. Don't put pressure on yourself to achieve your goals, but start with small steps! For example, start with a 10-minute run and then raise the bar higher and higher! You'll be surprised how you can run 100 minutes in a few weeks. When I was in London in the summer of 2019, I ran along the Thames three times a week in addition to my swimming training. I started slowly and set myself the goal of getting faster every week on the same route. After 10 weeks, I was faster and in better shape. The same goes for cold water: when I was training for the English and Northern Canal, I started with short cold showers of just 10 seconds. After 10 weeks, I could take cold showers for 10 minutes. All great things start with small, realistic steps to lay the foundation for bigger steps. I never thought I would write a book about my story, but that's the way it is. I started with small steps, like creating my own website, and writing my own blog, and now I've published my second book, which I hope will touch the hearts of people all over the world. There are no limits to what you can achieve outside of the boundaries you set for your own thinking.

3. **Face your fears!**

   Fears are a natural and important part of our personal development. Every time we consciously step out of our comfort zone, the next uncomfortable thing becomes a little easier and we know we can overcome our fears. Our fears stop us from taking another step forward. The more you face your fears, the more you realize that you can control your feelings and that your fears are a mindset that you can change. Ten years ago, I got hypothermia while swimming in cold water and ended up in hospital. As a result, I was terrified of cold water and felt uncomfortable in the cold. I swam in 3-degree cold water in Munich's Eisbach to build up my mental stamina and overcome my fear. I convinced my friends to look after me, and we all enjoyed the challenge. I have always been afraid of sharks, but despite this fear, I swam from Robben

Island to Cape Town, becoming the first Turkish woman to swim this iconic distance. These confrontational experiences showed me that I am stronger than my fears.

4. **Break your routine!**

   How can you discover yourself in a different way if you do the same thing every day? Take a different route to work, run in the opposite direction to your normal running route or pursue your hobby at a different time of day! Work in a different team or project and immerse yourself in new environments! This will allow you to think differently, be inspired by different circumstances and discover yourself in different situations. During the lockdown, it was a new normal routine with new colleagues and friends. With each new experience, both professionally and personally, I have come one step closer to my inner self. I have explored my qualities, strengths and weaknesses and feel more alive and grounded than ever.

5. **Let go of control and trust the process!**

   I'm a control freak, but I've learned that I can't control everything in my life. You can control your mind, your body, your emotions, what you eat, what you drink, what you do, where you work, who you talk to, etc., but there are also external factors that make life more complex and, at the same time, more interesting. I like the main rule of design thinking, an innovative, human-centered approach to finding solutions: "Trust the process!" Sometimes, you have to accept the unclear area of uncertainty – it can be good to let things go from time to time. Do everything you can, believe in what you are doing, but also be open to letting go and trusting the process. After all, magic can happen, just like the creative new ideas in the design thinking process. I don't know when I will be able to realize my postponed plans. But I believe that magic can happen at any moment and that everything in life has a reason. Calm down, accept the unknown and prepare for the next magical moments in your life!

6. **Try something new and accept something you wouldn't normally think of!**

   Take on a project that is not 100% in line with your expertise, or try out a new hobby or dish or participate in a weekend event with other people. Even if it doesn't work out in the end, experience is important. My sister is a part-time yoga teacher. She always asks me to attend different yoga camps with her. One weekend, I found myself at a unique yoga camp: everyone was dressed in white and focused. At first, I felt completely alien and tried to adapt to this different environment. Every unique experience shapes our thoughts and offers different perspectives. South Africa was not a place I had initially thought of. I wanted to go to Sydney, New York or Singapore, but once I was there, and it turned out to be a unique experience in my life that I am truly grateful for. Every restriction or challenge gives you the opportunity to try and discover something new in your life. Embrace this!

7. **Ask questions, even if they are unpleasant!**

   Don't be afraid to ask challenging and even childishly stupid questions! True to EY's motto: "The better the questions, the better the answers", ask yourself challenging questions and try to see things from a different perspective! Ask for feedback! Ask for what you want without hesitation! The fundamental question of "why" defines the purpose of every action. Stop and ask yourself why you do what you do and how you can improve yourself and others! Help the people around you to find their own answers, inside or outside their comfort zone! Don't stop yourself if others don't understand why you do something. If you don't know the answer yourself, keep thinking anyway! You will find your answer during the journey!

8. **Follow your passion!**

   Take the time to recognize your true passion. If you don't know yet, don't worry. Try out different things and think about how you feel. What is your source of energy? Where do you feel strong and happy? Find out what activities energize you and make you happier and stronger in your life. I feel more alive, stronger, and happier every time I swim. Such feelings show you what your true passion is. Imagine you had just one day to yourself, without work and other commitments. What would you want to do for yourself first?

9. **Go to new places and talk to strangers!**

   Don't be afraid to talk to people on the street, in the office or on the subway! Go to new places to meet people with different cultures or experiences! When you explore different and unknown places, you discover a different side of yourself. Be free, don't limit yourself, and you will see what surprises life offers you every day. Johannesburg was not a city I thought I would work and live in but the experience was great for me. I currently live in Zurich, and everything I have experienced here in the last two years has been incredible.

10. **Be mindful and know yourself**

    Mindfulness means you notice your thoughts, feelings, body reactions and surroundings in each moment with a gentle, nurturing gaze. By being mindful, you pay attention to your thoughts and feelings and accept them without judging them, e.g. without believing that there is a "right" or "wrong" way to think or feel in a particular moment. When we practice mindfulness, our thoughts focus on what we are feeling in the present moment rather than dipping into the past or imagining the future. You can start by increasing your mindfulness through meditation or even short self-reflection sessions. I started with the Wim Hof method, a combination of meditation, cold water applications, breathing and focusing, which helped me focus better and have the courage to step out of my comfort zone. During the lockdown, I started a comprehensive meditation guided by Dr Joe Dispenza, which helped me a lot in structuring my thoughts and, most importantly, understanding what I really want in life. Take time for self-reflection at least once a week, listen to your deep inner voice, accept what you feel and embrace yourself!

11. **It's all a question of attitude – enjoy the difficult moments!**

    Enjoy every moment, even if you feel challenged! Remind yourself to appreciate your journey and see all experiences as an opportunity to enjoy your life to the fullest! Sometimes, we feel tired and challenged, but it doesn't matter. You can still change your mindset and do what you need to do with a more positive attitude, and you will have more energy, be stronger and get more enjoyment out of what you are already doing.

12. **Life is short, cherish every moment and live life to the fullest!**

    This may sound trivial or normal to you, but I really mean it! Stop worrying about tomorrow! Problems or difficult situations will come one way or another, whether you worry about them or not. Just like the good things in your life. No matter what you think and do, good or bad things will happen in your life. If something is meant to happen, it will happen. You can't control everything in life. You can accept what happens and control your own reactions, emotions, and efforts to make things better so that you feel better. Stop worrying, just be grateful, accept and live the moment to the fullest. Appreciate every moment, the time you spend with your loved ones. Life is too short.

13. **Transform pain into creative energy – be the best version of yourself!**

The extraordinary thing is that each of us has the ability to rise like a phoenix from the ashes, recreate ourselves, and start again. Perhaps the true purpose of suffering is that we rise from our suffering, we develop, grow, and achieve.

14. **Where there is faith, there is no uncertainty. Discover your potential and trust in your own journey of discovery!**

    Your limits are your imagination. Despite your fears and inner obstacles, pursue your dream, follow your passion, work hard, take time for conscious renewal, and believe in yourself! Even if your mind tells you otherwise and your feelings express themselves in the form of fear. You are more than you think, and you will be surprised at what you are really capable of!

    Remember that your brain is your limit. Pursue your passion every day! Explore the world, discover yourself and step out of your comfort zone! Miracles will be waiting for you!

15. **Defeats are part of your journey to success!**

    Defeats are often an inevitable part of the success process. They can offer valuable lessons that help us improve, recognize our mistakes, and ultimately move forward stronger and wiser. It is important to see failures not as an end point but as an opportunity for further development. The ability to learn from defeats and not be discouraged by them can significantly contribute to achieving long-term success.

16. **Fear is your best friend**

    Fear is your compass that shows you the way to personal growth and change. It sparks creativity and makes life much more vibrant. Imagine a life without fear – how boring it would be! If you had no fear, what changes would you make today? What would you start doing?

This question alone can open new perspectives in your mind.

Paradoxically, fear is both your obstacle and your greatest ally. Even though fear may seem like a closed door, it is actually an open one. If you walk through this door, you can achieve more than you ever thought possible.

Remember: The more you venture beyond your comfort zone, the more self-confidence you gain! You expand your comfort zone, challenge your inner limits, and activate your learning and growth zones! Conquering the unknown empowers you to do great things!

All the love for you,

Deniz Kayadelen

Resources

BOOKS

- *Way of the Iceman: How the Wim Hof Method Creates Radiant, Long-term Health – Using the Science & Secrets of Breath Control, Cold-Training and Commitment*, Hof, Wim Hof. Dragon Door Publications, December 2016
- *The Wim Hof Method: Activate Your Potential, Transcend Your Limits.* Hof, Wim Hof. Ebury Digital, 1st edition September 2020
- *EY Expat Guidelines, Security Hints for South Africa, 2019*
- *Religions in the Modern World: Traditions and Transformations.* Woodhead, Linda, Partridge Christopher, Kawanami , Hiroko. Routledge, 3rd edition, January 2016

WEBSITES

- Meditation, Dr. Joe Dispenza, Blog https://blog.drjoedispenza.com/tag/meditation
- Accessing the Heart's Intelligence, Dr. Joe Dispenza, https://blog.drjoedispenza.com/blog/heart/accessing-the-hearts-intelligence
- 'Flow' Can Help You Achieve Goals Understanding the Psychology of Flow, By Kendra Cherry, Medically reviewed by Carly Snyder, MD on June 03, 2020, https://www.verywellmind.com/what-is-flow-2794768
- Guided Wim Hof Method Breathing – YouTube https://www.youtube.com/watch?v=tybOi4hjZFQ

- How "brown fat" helps you cope with cold weather, By Hanna Ali, Sunday, December 29, 2019 NOVA Next https://www.pbs.org/wgbh/nova/article/brown-fat-cold-weather/
- Cape Long Distance Swim Association, South Africa, https://cldsa.co.za/
- English Channel Swim Association, https://www.channelswimmingassociation.com/
- North Channel Swim Association, https://northchannelswimming.com/index.html
- Out of Our Comfort Zone, www.outofourcomfortzone.com
- Oceanman https://oceanman-openwater.com/
- The Wealth Hike, The Comfort Zone, by @ thewealthhike https://www.thewealthhike.com/blog
- Ryan Stamrood, https://ryanstramrood.com/
- Cross Continental Swimming Race, Istanbul http://bogazici.olimpiyatkomitesi.org.tr/
- "10 Ways to step out of your comfort zone" https://www.lifehack.org/articles/communication/10-ways-step-out-your-comfort-zone-and-enjoy-taking-risks.html
- The best swimming lakes around Frankfurt | Bike Touring https://www.komoot.com/collection/141/the-best-swimming-lakes-around-frankfurt
- The Way Of The Iceman | Download [Pdf]/[ePub] eBook. https://www.getsfreebook.com/gets/the-way-of-the-iceman
- What are the Benefits of Cold Showers? | Wim Hof Method. https://www.wimhofmethod.com/benefits-of-cold-showers
- How to Use the Power of Visualization - Mindvalley Blog. https://blog.mindvalley.com/the-power-of-visualization/
- Healthy Fat' Foods for Your Diet - WebMD. https://www.webmd.com/diet/ss/slideshow-healthy-fat-foods

- What Are The Benefits of Sleeping More? - SelfGrowth.com. https://www.selfgrowth.com/articles/what-are-the-benefits-of-sleeping-more
- About Cryo Treatments – Delray Beach Cryo. https://delraybeachcryo.com/about-cryo-treatments/
- Change management and experience services | EY - US. https://www.ey.com/en_us/workforce/change-management-experience
- Safety Tips for Tourists - Umhlanga Rocks Tourism Safety .... https://umhlangatourism.com/tourist-information-umhlanga-umhlanga-rocks-tourism/safety-tips-for-tourists-umhlanga-rocks-tourism/
- 20 Rules for Safe Travel in South Africa - Transitions Abroad. https://www.transitionsabroad.com/listings/travel/articles/safety-rules-for-travel-in-south-africa.shtml

About the Author

DENIZ KAYADELEN is a multicultural business psychologist of Turkish descent who grew up in Germany. She is not only a world champion in ice swimming, but also a successful entrepreneur and head of Talent Management Consulting at EY. Deniz crossed the English Channel Solo in 2023 and became 5 times World Champion in IISA Ice Swimming.

As the founder of Out of Comfort Zone, Deniz has received numerous awards for her inspiring speeches, including from Forbes, Tedx, and the NY Journal. With over 12 years of experience connecting business and psychology in over 5 countries, as well as over 20 years of experience as a swimming coach, Deniz has unique expertise in helping individuals and organizations bring out the best in themselves. She shares her experiences and helps others unlock their potentials and find self-fulfillment.

Instagram:
@swimmerpsychologist
@outofcomfortzone_dk

Linkedin:
www.linkedin.com/in/denizkayadelen/

Webpage:
www.outofourcomfortzone.com/

Mail:
info@outofourcomfortzone.com

Thank You

Thank You For Reading My Book!

I really appreciate all of your feedback, and I love hearing what you have to say.

I need your input to make the next version of this book and my future books even better.

Please leave me a helpful review on Amazon letting me know what you thought of the book.

Thank you so much!
Deniz Kayadelen

Printed in Great Britain
by Amazon

59552030R00126